The Diary of
Caroline Seabury
1854–1863

Wisconsin Studies in American Autobiography

WILLIAM L. ANDREWS
General Editor

The Diary of

Caroline Seabury

1854–1863

Edited with an Introduction by

Suzanne L. Bunkers

THE UNIVERSITY OF WISCONSIN PRESS

The University of Wisconsin Press
114 North Murray Street
Madison, Wisconsin 53715

3 Henrietta Street
London WC2E 8LU, England

Published with permission of the Minnesota Historical Society.
The original Caroline Seabury diary is housed in the Channing Seabury
and Family Papers, Minnesota Historical Society, St. Paul, Minnesota.

Library of Congress Cataloging-in-Publication Data
Seabury, Caroline, 1827–1893.
The diary of Caroline Seabury, 1854–1863 / edited with an
introduction by Suzanne L. Bunkers.
162 pp.   cm. – (Wisconsin studies in American autobiography)
Includes bibliographical references.
1. Southern States – Social life and customs – 1775–1865.
2. Mississippi – Social life and customs. 3. Slavery – Southern
States – History – 19th century. 4. Slavery – Mississippi –
History – 19th century. 5. United States – History – Civil War,
1861–1865 – Personal narratives. 6. Mississippi – History – Civil War,
1861–1865 – Personal narratives. 7. Seabury, Caroline, 1827–1893 –
Diaries. 8. Teachers – Mississippi – Columbus – Diaries. 9. Columbus
(Miss.) – Biography. I. Bunkers, Suzanne L.
II. Title. III. Series.
F213.S42   1991
976.2'973 – dc20
ISBN 0-299-12870-9   90-50640
ISBN 0-299-12874-1 (pbk.)   CIP

"Our object in this labor is to make a usable past, to make the cloak of history wearable so our daughters may fling it over their shoulders and go off on tracks of their own"
—Jane Marcus, "Invisible Mending"

for
Edith, Sally, and
Rachel Susanna

Contents

Acknowledgments
vii

Introduction
3

THE DIARY OF CAROLINE SEABURY
23

Notes
123

Bibliography
139

Index
142

Acknowledgments
❦

I am deeply appreciative of the support which many individuals and organizations have provided as I have worked on this project. Ruth Bauer, Reading Room supervisor and archivist at the Minnesota Historical Society Research Center, first brought the manuscript diary of Caroline Seabury to my attention. Susan Hill Gross, director of the Upper Midwest Women's History Center for Teachers, Central Community Center, St. Louis Park, Minnesota, referred me to a series of teaching units on women in Minnesota history. K. G. Woods, Shiela C. Robertson, and Kathleen Ann O'Brien's intermediate social studies unit on Caroline Seabury opened the door for my investigation into the diarist's life and writings.

In reconstructing Caroline's life, I have located and analyzed census records, city directories, newspaper obituaries, state death records, and cemetery plat books, but I have not worked alone. Genealogists Shirley Pizziferri and Marjorie McMaster combed Massachusetts records for information on Caroline's ancestry. Carolyn Neault, librarian in the Lowndes County Library System in Columbus, Mississippi, helped me piece together details of Caroline's years there. Samuel H. Kaye provided information on the Columbus Female Institute and on individuals mentioned in the diary. Mickey Croce helped me verify historical references in the diary. Dallas Lindgren, head of Reference Services at the Minnesota Historical Society, assisted me in securing permission to publish the Seabury diary. Ruth Bauer and Steven Nielsen, archivists at the Minnesota Historical Society, helped me locate information in city directories and arranged for photographs of individual diary pages. Bonnie Wilson, curator of the Audio-Visual Library of the

Minnesota Historical Society, provided photographs of Caroline and Channing Seabury to accompany the diary text. Edith Seabury Nye and Sally Seabury Cole, Channing Seabury's daughter and great-granddaughter, encouraged me to publish Caroline's diary, which they had not known existed.

Transforming a handwritten nineteenth-century diary into a book has required a good deal of faith and effort, not only on my part but also on the parts of others. Kathleen Kea spent many hours carefully verifying details and preparing an accurate typescript of the diary. Margo Culley provided a thoughtful and helpful reader's report on my manuscript. William Andrews, general editor of the University of Wisconsin Press's series on American autobiography, accepted the diary for publication in the series and provided valuable feedback as I prepared the introduction. Barbara Hanrahan, humanities editor at the University of Wisconsin Press, guided the manuscript through the publication process. Raphael Kadushin, Carol Olsen, and Sylvan Esh offered valuable editorial direction, and Angela Ray read the typescript closely and carefully. The National Endowment for the Humanities, the American Council of Learned Societies, and Mankato State University provided generous funding to underwrite my research. An honorary fellowship at the University of Wisconsin–Madison Women's Studies Research Center gave me added impetus to complete my work.

James Olney and the members of his 1983 NEH summer seminar on "The Forms of Autobiography" first encouraged me to consider the diary as autobiography. Lynn Bloom, Rebecca Hogan, Cynthia Huff, Judy Lensink, and Trudelle Thomas helped me gain many highly useful insights into female diarists' purposes, intended audiences, and writing techniques.

My colleagues at Mankato State University have been consistently supportive of my work. My students in several theory of autobiography and women's autobiography classes eagerly read and discussed countless diaries with me. My family and friends helped me gather the stamina and conviction needed to bring this project to fruition. My cousin Frank Klein furnished a quiet cabin in the woods where I worked on the manuscript. My daughter, Rachel Susanna, waited patiently while I fed one more bit of data into the computer or checked endnotes one final time, then suggested that we go outside and play.

For these individuals' contributions, I am grateful. The diary of Caroline Seabury could not have been published without their assistance.

The Diary of
Caroline Seabury
1854–1863
❧

Introduction

1854 Christmas . . . The hum-drum life of a teacher gives
little variety save what one's own thoughts afford. I think
as my journey has been noted down, for the first time in
my life, I will keep a sort of journal, perhaps not [to] be
seen once in three months, but when I feel like scribbling
it may help to while away time, perhaps now & then something may happen which I will like to look over in after
years—my sister & I together. We can jot down in short
hand & enlarge at our leisure. As another has said, "it may
string the pearls that, otherwise lying loose, might be trodden upon and swept away."—If there are no pearls to string
in our lives, "it will recall events & feelings which might
else be forgotten."

CAROLINE SEABURY wrote these words in her diary shortly
after leaving Brooklyn, New York, in October 1854, and ar-
riving in Columbus, Mississippi.[1] There she took a position
as a French teacher at the Columbus Female Institute, a school
for the daughters of well-to-do white citizens of the area. A
native of Southbridge, Massachusetts, Caroline was one of
three surviving members of the Seabury family, eight of whom
had died from consumption. Like many white, middle-class
American women, twenty-seven-year-old Caroline Seabury
needed to support herself, and teaching was one of the few
professions open to women during the mid-1800s.[2] Not sur-
prisingly, she became a teacher.

Instead of remaining in her native New England, Seabury
decided to journey to a place far different from what she had
known all her life. This decision was to play a crucial role in
how and what she wrote in her diary during the next nine

years. In it, she recorded her uneasiness as a white Northerner living in the American South and observing what she called the "peculiar institution" of slavery. Caroline stayed in Mississippi for nearly a decade before fleeing back to the North at the height of the Civil War. Her diary ended upon her return to the North.

The diary was donated to the Minnesota Historical Society in 1955 by descendants of Caroline's younger brother, Channing Seabury, who had served as chairman of the Minnesota Board of State Capitol Commissioners from 1893 to 1908. Perhaps the diary was deemed noteworthy because it focused on an important era in American history, perhaps because it was written by the sister of a well-known figure in Minneosta politics. Whatever the reason, the diary was accepted by the Minnesota Historical Society and cataloged as part of the Channing Seabury and Family Papers. The information file accompanying the collection describes Channing Seabury's life and then concludes with this cryptic sentence: "No information could be located on Caroline Seabury, Channing's sister."

Today Caroline Seabury's manuscript diary survives as an important document of life in the American South during the Civil War era. It is especially illuminating for today's readers as a record of one woman's uneasy attempts to come to terms with her position as an unmarried white Northern woman whose job it was to educate wealthy white Southern girls in an environment seemingly oblivious to the horrors of slavery.

Piecing together the details of Caroline Seabury's life has been a challenging, exhilarating, and sometimes frustrating process. It can be compared to trying to put together a jigsaw puzzle when several of the pieces are nowhere to be found. It can be likened to sewing a patchwork quilt, using up whatever fabric one has on hand, then waiting to receive other bits and pieces that can be stitched into place.[3]

My gathering of biographical information on Caroline Seabury has been done as time has permitted. I made regular trips to the Minnesota Historical Society Research Center, where

Caroline Seabury, photographed while she was living in St. Paul, Minnesota. Courtesy of the Minnesota Historical Society.

I studied reel after reel of microfilmed city directory records, census records, and newspaper stories. I visited the Minnesota Office of Vital Statistics, searching for clues concerning where and when Caroline died. I corresponded regularly with Seabury descendants, hoping that they could provide some clues about how Caroline, the ancestor they never knew, had lived out her life. I drove slowly through Oakland Cemetery in St. Paul (my two-year-old daughter napping in her baby seat in our car), looking for the Seabury family plot. I sat in my attic study late into the night with all my notecards spread out on the floor before me, pondering where to go next in my search to learn more about Caroline.

In good time the bits and pieces of information began to come together, and I realized that I had learned as much about Caroline Seabury as I was likely to, given my own time constraints and my publisher's desire to get her diary into print. What follows is not intended to represent the "whole picture." Rather, it is intended to present those parts of the jigsaw puzzle, those carefully cut and pieced portions of the patchwork quilt, that have thus far been assembled.[4]

On both the maternal and paternal sides, Caroline Seabury's family had deep roots in Massachusetts.[5] Her father, John Seabury, the son of Joseph and Rebecca Seabury, was born in Eastham on February 4, 1790. Like his father, John Seabury became a physician. He set up his practice in Chatham, where he married his first wife, Maria Plimpton, the daughter of Oliver Plimpton and Lydia Fiske Plimpton. Maria died in 1824 after giving birth to three children – Julia, Lucretia, and Maria.

In 1825 John Seabury married Caroline Plimpton, the first cousin of his deceased wife Maria. Caroline, the fifth child of Gershom Plimpton and Keziah Fiske, was born in Sturbridge on September 18, 1803. After their marriage, John and Caroline Seabury made their home in Southbridge, where six children – Caroline, John, Mary, Helen, Martha, and Channing – were born to them. Julia, Lucretia, and Maria Seabury continued to make their home with their father and stepmother.

Caroline Russell Seabury, the first child of John and Caroline Plimpton Seabury, was born on June 1, 1827, in Southbridge. Little is known about Caroline's childhood except that during those years eight family members died of consumption, one of the most virulent diseases of the nineteenth century.[6] In April 1850 Caroline's younger sister Mary died of the disease, and three months later, on July 11, 1850, Caroline's mother committed suicide at the age of forty-six.[7] Information concerning the death of Caroline Plimpton Seabury's husband, John Seabury, has not yet been found; at the time of her death in 1850, however, Caroline was listed as a widow.[8] Three children—Caroline, Martha, and Channing—survived their parents.

During her early years, Caroline the younger no doubt attended school—quite likely one of the female seminaries operating in Massachusetts at the time. The female seminary (sometimes known as the female institute or academy) came into existence in the United States as early as 1814, when Emma Willard opened the Middlebury Female Seminary. Other similar institutions soon followed. Their purpose was to provide educational opportunities for young women beyond the common schooling available to them as girls. The typical curriculum at a female institute comprised courses in literature, languages, philosophy, history, mathematics, and the sciences.[9] It is evident from Caroline's diary that she knew Latin and French well and that she had studied the works of Shakespeare and other major writers. By the early 1850s Caroline, her sister Martha, and their younger brother Channing were in the care of their mother's brother, Edwin Plimpton, and his wife, Mary Hastings, of Brooklyn, New York. Edwin Plimpton was a businessman, and the letters which Channing and Caroline wrote to him and his wife many years later reveal that they stayed in contact and enjoyed a good relationship with their uncle and aunt's family.

As her diary indicates, Caroline doubtless recognized the necessity of making a living and supporting herself. In October 1854, when she began her journey to Columbus, Mississippi, Caroline was a twenty-seven-year-old single woman newly hired as a teacher of French at the recently reorganized Columbus Female Institute. The institute, first organized in 1847, was situated in a large twelve-room house, and it began accepting students in 1848.[10] Caroline's new teaching position offered her the opportunity to explore a part of the world that she had never seen and to live in a culture unfamiliar to her. Perhaps more important, it provided her for the first time in her life with some degree of financial security and independence.[11]

On October 7, 1854, Caroline and her traveling companions left Brooklyn by ferry and began their long journey to Columbus, Mississippi. Along the way she made shorthand notes, which she later transformed into her first journal entry of seventeen pages. In this initial entry, she described the South as "the land of flowers, fanned by gentle breezes—they who have written of it tell us there is sweetness every-where." Of her purpose in going there, she said, "I am going to learn what among them is the life of a 'Yankee teacher.'" She saw her journey as the beginning of a new life, writing: "I was leaving a sad gloomy sorrow marked past—going to an untried future, & could only 'let the dead past bury its dead,' hoping for a brighter future, of contented usefulness at least." Upon her arrival in Columbus, Caroline went to the Columbus Female Institute, where she met its president, the Reverend R. A. Means, who lived there with his wife and their two daughters. Caroline's early diary entries reflect her understanding of class differences and of her nonprivileged position as an unmarried woman teacher.

Caroline's startling obliviousness to the realities of slavery—and her prejudices concerning people of color—took longer to dissipate. On November 18, 1854, Caroline wrote, "I see little of the effect of slavery—in fact, nothing except the everyday life of servants. All we have heard of its horrors may be true—they seem a happy, careless thoughtless race." Not until February 1855 did she witness firsthand the cruelties inflicted on black slaves by white masters. On February 8, 1855, Caroline wrote a lengthy description of what she called the "first illustration" of the "peculiar institution of the South." From her upstairs room, Caroline could hear the master whipping the "maid-of-all-work Milly" in the cellar of the institute, ostensibly for stealing money from one of the young white girls boarding there. Caroline shut her door but could not banish Milly's screams from her mind.

Two days later, Caroline wrote that Milly had been exonerated when the daughter of a rich planter confessed to having stolen the money. Subsequent diary entries tell of seeing a recaptured runaway slave who had been badly beaten, of watching a horrifying slave auction in which a young mother was stripped of her children and sold to the highest bidder, and of witnessing the arrival of a slave ship from Africa.

Despite the loss of her innocence and her horror at seeing the endless abuses of the system of slavery, Caroline learned to keep her views to herself. As a white Northern woman, unmarried and living solely on her income from teaching white Southern girls, she was in a precarious position. As her diary entries make clear, she felt invisible and silenced, yet she was unable to silence herself completely.

Caroline originally intended her diary to be a joint record of her sister Martha's and her experiences in the South, as she noted in her Christmas 1854 entry, made on the day Martha arrived in Columbus to teach with Caroline.[12] The Seabury sisters' first years in Columbus apparently went well. Diary entries indicate that they liked living there and made friends in the community. Still, they could not ignore the horrors of slavery that surrounded them. The diary became the one safe place for recording evidence of these cruelties; it was a document which the sisters planned to reread in later years as a lasting reminder of their sojourn in the South.

During the spring of 1857 Caroline cared for a young boy, John Dupree, who had come down with smallpox. Later the townspeople rewarded her for her efforts by giving her a silver service and other gifts. This incident gave Caroline a sense of belonging to the community, yet it did not allay her terrible loneliness and sense of homelessness. Caroline's worries were compounded by her own bouts with illness as well as by her sister Martha's fragile health. In January 1858 Martha began hemorrhaging from her lungs—a sure sign of consumption. On June 7, 1858, Martha died. The Columbus townspeople donated a burial plot for Martha in Friendship Cemetery. Caroline, griefstricken, spent many hours visiting her sister's grave.

Caroline wrote little in her diary during the year that followed. In the fall of 1858 the Columbus Female Institute had to close its doors after its dormitory was destroyed in a fire. It would not reopen until October 1860. In October 1859 Caroline returned to Columbus after spending the summer with her brother Channing and their Plimpton relatives in Manchester, Vermont.[13] In the fall of 1861 Caroline made a trip to New York. When she returned to Columbus to resume teaching that fall, she drew the cloak of nineteenth-century True Womanhood tightly around her, trying hard to convince herself that she was not accountable for the evils of slavery.

While Caroline heartily disapproved of the approaching war and of the suffering it would bring to both Northerners and Southerners, she was determined to make herself useful by helping those who were suffering—perhaps in the bargain hoping to gain that sense of self-worth and feeling of belonging for which she yearned. Once the Civil War began in April 1861, Caroline Seabury used her journal to report specific battles, to discuss townspeople's adjustments to a wartime economy, to describe her work as a volunteer nurse to Confederate wounded, and to record her conflicting feelings about the war. In 1862 Caroline lost her teaching position when the principal at the Columbus Female Institute decided to employ only Southerners as teachers. In need of a means of self-support, Caroline found work tutoring the daughters of Colonel George Hampton Young, owner of Waverly Plantation near Columbus.[14]

The summer of 1863 brought the siege of Vicksburg and its surrender of Confederate forces to the Union army on July 4. Caroline was desperate to return to the North, to leave what she called a "desolate country" behind. On July 28, 1863, after the Union forces had broken through Confederate lines, Caroline wrote that an "unexpected opportunity" to return to the North had come her way. On July 29 she undertook a difficult trip toward the Mississippi River by covered wagon, driven by a Mr. Stone, a Southerner with sympathies for the Union. He was assisted by an Irishman named Dan and a slave named Jack. Caroline wrote in her diary of the land laid waste, of destitute farming families, of incredibly high prices for scarce goods, and of sick and wounded people she met along the way. At one point in the journey, she recounted the words of a poor woman at whose home they stopped for water: "This is the rich folks'es war."

Eventually her group reached the Mississippi River, where, after fashioning a homemade Union flag, Caroline waved down a passing boat, the *Moderator,* carrying Union soldiers returning from Vicksburg. She was able to arrange for safe passage to Memphis. From there she booked passage by boat to Cairo, Illinois, then went on to Cincinnati by train. After spending ten days visiting her cousins there, she continued by train to Brooklyn, where she returned to Edwin and Maria Plimpton's home. Ironically, they were not at home when she arrived, and she had to get the house key from their neighbors. Sitting in their home on August 27, 1863, Caroline wrote a somber concluding entry in her diary.

Little is known about Caroline Seabury's life during the thirty years after she returned to the North from Mississippi. Letters in the Channing Seabury and Family papers, written by Caroline and her brother Channing to their aunt and uncle, Edwin and Maria Plimpton, reveal that by 1866 Caroline had gone to live with Channing in St. Paul, where she kept house for him until his first marriage to Frances Warren Cruft in 1870. During those years Caroline cooked and raised flowers, did the bookkeeping for Channing's wholesale grocery business, and occasionally traveled east to visit her relatives. She apparently stayed in touch with some of the friends she had made in Columbus: one letter to the Plimptons (dated September 23,

Channing Seabury. Courtesy of the Minnesota Historical Society.

The Seabury residence in St. Paul, Minnesota, circa 1890. Courtesy of the Minnesota Historical Society.

1866) mentions that her friends, the Christians, were visiting from the South. Her health was apparently somewhat fragile: in one of his letters to the Plimptons (dated March 28, 1866), Channing noted that Caroline was having a hard time breathing and had to stay indoors a lot. It is unclear whether Caroline continued to live with Channing and Frances during their marriage. St. Paul city directories show that, following Frances's death in 1878, Caroline was living with her brother and helping him raise his children, Charles and John.[15] Channing's son Charles died in December 1882, and in 1883 Channing married Elizabeth Austin of Milwaukee, Wisconsin. They and Channing's son John continued to live in St.

Paul, although Caroline did not live with them. During the next decade Elizabeth gave birth to four children: Gerald, Austin, Paul, and Edith Seabury.[16] Channing Seabury died on October 28, 1910, and Elizabeth Austin Seabury died on April 16, 1944.[17]

Caroline's niece, Edith Seabury Nye, recalls having heard from her mother, Elizabeth Austin Seabury, that Caroline had left St. Paul during the 1880s and had gone to live somewhere in the South.[18] Vital statistics records show that Caroline Seabury died on March 18, 1893, in Washington, D.C., where she had been living for five months.[19] Her body was returned to St. Paul for burial in the Seabury family plot in Oakland Cemetery near the state capitol.

The diary of Caroline Seabury is a significant historical record that chronicles a major era in American history from the perspective of a woman who saw herself as an outsider in Southern culture as well as an orphan in search of a home and family. The diary traces Caroline's development from a naive observer to a woman with deeply divided loyalties and a great deal of empathy for the sufferings of both Northerners and Southerners during a turbulent time in our nation's history. It registers her feelings of helplessness as a bystander who was nonetheless implicated in the abuse of human beings sanctioned by the institution of slavery. It reveals to present-day readers the convoluted psychological make-up of a slave-owning culture. At the same time, it asks readers to examine the daily life of a woman who would never become an insider in Southern society. It is a text that defies easy classification because of the insightfulness of its author, whose dual perspective (that of insider/outsider) is virtually unrepresented in published personal narratives dating from the Civil War era.

For all these reasons, the diary of Caroline Seabury is well worth studying as a historical artifact. It is also an important contribution to the field of American autobiography, for it represents the synthesis of several key elements of personal nar-

Caroline Seabury's tombstone

rative that are rarely seen in combination. As a diarist, Caroline recorded her selected impressions of life in the Civil War–era South. She did not write brief daily entries; instead, she wrote lengthier entries based on significant life experiences, the memories of which she wanted to preserve for future rereading. Her customary method of writing was to jot down notes in shorthand while a particular experience was taking place, then take time later to expand and embellish those notes into longhand entries.

Caroline Seabury's diary helps to disprove the once commonly held assumption that the diary was an extremely private, secretive text, particularly for a woman. As Caroline stated in her Christmas 1854 entry, she began keeping a diary not only to "help to while away time" but also to keep a record that she and her sister Martha might reread in later years to remind them of their experiences in the South. Thus Caroline's diary, like those kept by many nineteenth-century women, was undertaken as a collaborative text. Such diaries functioned as family documents, written for audiences wider than the diarist alone. An understanding of Caroline Seabury's purpose and intended audience is therefore important in interpreting what Caroline Seabury wrote in her diary as well as what she didn't write. Her diary functioned not only as a family record but also, I would assert, as a trusted confidante and family member, especially after the death of her sister Martha.[20]

In many respects, the diary of Caroline Seabury became what Robert Fothergill calls a "book of the self."[21] As Caroline continued to write in her diary over a period of nine years, it began to take shape as a life narrative which recorded her experiences and reflected upon their significance. Her choice of a hard-covered, lined diary with bound and numbered pages is evidence that she thought of her diary as a permanent record of her experiences. Her practice of pasting newspaper clippings, photographs, sketches, and memorabilia onto the diary's pages further contributed to her shaping of the diary into a book. Her story, framed by two journeys—from Brooklyn to Columbus in 1854 and from Columbus back to Brooklyn in 1863—can be read as an odyssey of an individual's progress from innocence to experience. More specifically, it can be read as the story of one woman's growing awareness of the complexities of attitude and behavior in a nineteenth-century culture about which she felt extremely ambivalent.

Robert Fothergill writes about the tendency of many diarists to take great care with their diaries, writing neatly and binding the volumes handsomely (45). As Fothergill concludes, the question of whether or not a diarist begins his or her text with the intention of its becoming a life narrative is not what determines whether the diary becomes a "book of the self." Often that process happens organically as the diary develops and the writer becomes aware of its function as a creation and reflection of self.[22] In such cases, the diary becomes what Fothergill calls "serial autobiography," that is, a shaped narrative that "links one's days together and makes them significant and interesting" (153). Caroline Seabury's diary represents this type of serial autobiography by virtue of its continual selection and shaping of detail into a pattern of episodes in the life of its writer.

Reading and interpreting the diary of Caroline Seabury is fascinating and complicated for a twentieth-century reader living in a decidedly different historical context from that in which Caroline wrote. My perspective as reader/interpreter derives from my own experiences of race, class, ethnicity, and geographical setting. I need to beware of any tendency to view Caroline as a "typical" nineteenth-century American woman, since no one woman can be said to typify all women. I need to refrain from justifying or condemning her attitudes and actions based on my own belief system. Finally, I need to remember that the lens through which she viewed the world was a complex product of her perception of herself as a "lone woman" and an outsider; this perspective contributed significantly to what she wrote (and didn't write) in her journal.

Caroline's perception of being on her own in the world was essentially a valid one. She had no parents, siblings, or spouse on whom she could rely for financial or emotional support. Even her uncle's offer to provide for her as long as he lived would have given her a very tenuous sort of security. The reality of being a single white woman in nineteenth-century America meant that Caroline needed to find a way to support herself. While teaching could provide a woman with some measure of autonomy, a teacher's wages were meager and her status low, as Caroline observed in her diary. In effect, her decision to go to Mississippi (motivated by a desire to be of service as well as by financial considerations) meant leaving behind any semblance of home that she had ever known.

Caroline's adaptation to life in the South necessitated a continual mediation between her desire to create a home, family, and circle of friends and her growing understanding of the ugly abuses of human beings enslaved in that culture. As a white woman and as a teacher, she clearly had certain privileges that a woman who was black and a slave could never have hoped to attain. As a Northern woman, Caroline arrived in Mississippi with little understanding of the realities of the antagonistic yet mutually dependent relationships between black and white Southern women or of the magnitude of the white male Southerner's power over them.[23] Her journal became the place where she named the reality of the horrors which she witnessed and, paradoxically, where she tried her hardest to distance herself from any involvement in or responsibility for the perpetuation of those horrors. Caroline's diary reflects the many paradoxes and contradictions involved in her search for both a personal and a cultural home.

Like any individual, Caroline was a product of her time and place. Her racial prejudice is apparent in her stereotyping of the slaves whom she saw standing along the riverbank during her journey to the South as well as in her imitation of black dialect in describing the wedding of Charles and Maria at Waverly. Yet the great sympathy which she felt for human beings brutalized by those wielding the power of the "peculiar institution" is evident in her detailed descriptions of Milly's and Suey's plights. Caroline's journal served as an arena in which she could register her condemnation of the evils of slavery. At the same time it served as a friend to whom she could confide her sense of individual impotence as an outsider implicated in the injustices of slavery.

Along with many other white women living in the United States during the mid-1800s, Caroline Seabury was engaged in the dynamic of conforming to the Victorian ideology of True Womanhood while at the same time questioning the restrictions imposed on her by that ideology. She was expected to embody the four cardinal virtues of piety, purity, submissiveness, and domesticity.[24] As an unmarried woman, she was in a particularly precarious position—expected to remain in woman's "proper sphere" and at the same time to support herself. Caroline's role as a teacher in a female institute was equally problematic. Generally, unmarried women were employed as teachers of young girls, yet the role of the teacher was to perpetuate cultural ideals concerning women's place within the home and nuclear family.[25] Caroline was expected to serve as a stern but loving parental figure and to be a model of "proper" womanhood for her students. She had some degree of authority over her students, yet she remained subservient to the wishes of their parents and her own supervisors as well as dependent on the wages they paid her. Finally, as a Northerner in the South during the Civil War, Caroline's teaching position ultimately offered her no security, a reality she faced in 1862 when the principal of the Columbus Female Institute decided to employ only teachers of Southern birth and dismissed her.

All these complex factors make the diary of Caroline Seabury a striking historical and autobiographical text. Caroline shaped her text into a life narrative that derived its form and content from her perceptions of herself and of those around her. As she selected feelings, attitudes, and experiences to chronicle in her diary, Caroline created a story in which her personal situation echoed and mirrored larger issues of national identity and destiny. Like the diaries of Caroline's contemporaries Mary Chesnut, Charlotte L. Forten, Esther Hill Hawks, Hannah Ropes, Madge Preston, and Emily Hawley Gillespie, the diary of Caroline Seabury cannot be easily labeled and wedged into a little niche on a shelf. It is a text that raises challenging interpretive questions, not only about details of its author's life but also about her perspectives on her experiences.

The relationship between Caroline as writer of the text and myself as reader is interactive: as I edit Caroline's diary for publication, I interpret it and, by so doing, participate in the creation of meaning, just as does any other reader/interpreter of her diary.[26] Since the diary was written more than 130 years ago, I could not have been Caroline's intended reader. This does not mean, however, that I am an uninformed, uninvolved reader, for I bring to my study of her diary my own expertise as a writer of diaries and my own interpretive powers as a reader of literature. It also does not mean that my interpretation of Caroline's attitudes and experiences, as reflected in her diary, is set in stone. In the five years since I first read her diary, my knowledge of details of the author's life has increased, and my perspective on her experiences has deepened and broadened a great deal not only as a result of what I have learned about her but also as a result of what I have learned about myself. The context in which I read and reread, interpret and reinterpret, the diary of Caroline Seabury is reflexive and dynamic – it is process rather than product.[27] It represents my own negotiation of a variety of complex issues, and it reinforces my belief that the cryptic sentence in the papers describing the Seabury collection, "No information could be located on Caroline Seabury, Channing's sister," does not tell the whole story.

The 8½″ × 11″ hardbound diary, of dark green leather with maroon trim, contains approximately 150 pages of handwritten text plus newspaper clippings, samples of United States and Confederate currency, photographs of Abraham Lincoln and Jefferson Davis, and other Civil War memorabilia. My goal has been to reproduce the text of Caroline Seabury's diary as faithfully and as accurately as possible. I have retained the original capitalization, punctuation, spelling, and phrasing, even in the case of misspelling or misphrasing. I have added information in brackets when necessary to clarify meaning or supply missing letters or punctuation marks; all parenthetical information in the text was placed there by the author. I have retained the entire text of the diary; all ellipses were placed in the text by its author. I have added explanatory notes where appropriate to aid readers in identifying individuals, places, and events mentioned in the diary.

My objective in preparing the diary for publication has been to maintain the integrity of the text by presenting Caroline Seabury's diary as she wrote it rather than by condensing or censoring it according to any predetermined set of literary and/

or moral standards. In addition, my research into the diarist's life and environment has been undertaken and presented with an eye toward clarifying and explaining, not justifying or condemning, Caroline Seabury's beliefs and actions. Nonetheless, I recognize that my work as a reader, interpreter, and editor has not taken place in a vacuum. My own attitudes and experiences have influenced not only the way in which I have prepared the diary for publication but also my interest in it as historical record and life narrative. Thus, the text which you see here represents an interactive process, one that is not, cannot, and should not be value free.

THE DIARY

of Caroline Seabury

From Brooklyn to Columbus, Miss. –

October 7th, 1854 – The cold winds of early autumn are whistling
about us, driving before them the faded leaves, the flowers
have nearly all said their good-bye and gone. I have just
started for a long journey to the far South. My partings are
all over – at Jersey City Ferry with a world of strangers before – stranger to my traveling companions – stranger to the
people among whom my lot is to be cast. It is far-famed as
the land of flowers, fanned by gentle breezes – they who
have written of it tell us there is sweetness every-where. I
am going to learn what among them is the life of a "Yankee
teacher" – with a young lady going for the same purpose, a
gentleman, under whose care we travel, & a nephew of his
who is making his first long journey.[1] At five we P.M. we
started. Governor's Island lay in the glorious light of an
unclouded sunset as we took our last look of the last familiar object. "It may be for years and it may be forever." It
calls up a thousand thoughts of those we leave, of those
who have left us, for a land where no sorrow comes, there
is a shrinking from anything which disturbs our reveries –
but, soon, our quiet is over, we are hurried on board the
Philadelphia cars. The first feeling of being utter strangers
to each other soon passed away. As one thing after another
called forth little expressions from each of us – and night
soon came which seems to equalize all travelers' feelings
wonderfully – We had every requisite for a pleasant journey
– pleasant company, faultless weather & fast traveling.
There was no change until we reached Philadelphia, &
rushed to the next train, bound for Baltimore – again to
hurry on. The moon rose at her full, & many pretty spots
appeared as we whizzed by, crossing the beautiful Susque-
hanna was our only time for any enjoyment of the scenery
– & that was done on a crowded boat – with every-body in
a hurry to get over & such racing at break-neck speed after
we touched the banks – all, old & young running as if for
dear life to secure a comfortable seat for the night – we were
successful, and at one on Sunday morning heard the "all
aboard for Washington" sounded. Another rush – jam, pell-

The first page of Caroline Seabury's diary. Courtesy of the Minnesota Historical Society.

mell confusion & in ten minutes we were off again. It was a frosty night which made the thought of going South particularly pleasant. Two lively little Frenchmen just in front of us kept up a ceaseless talk—which increased in tones as their eau de vie was often brought to light. No nation certainly makes a greater show of happiness whether in reality

it is beyond that of our "universal Yankee nation" or not.
As they told an incident of a trip across the ocean the last
summer, the ludicrousness of which overpowered me, as
well as themselves, they turned round, & with a "pardon-
nez moi–vous comprenez Français, madamoiselle," they
lowered the tones which had kept us all awake. We were
dozing stupidly with the chills, which come to those who
are out all night chasing each other over our material selves,
when the conductor came through the car uttering–Washington. The moon was growing pale, daylight was stealing
over the earth again, as we first caught sight of our great
capitol in the distance. At sunrise we were riding down
Pennsylvania Avenue, past the White House, Smithsonian
Institute and the great National Monument to the memory of our beloved Washington. It has been built by contributions from all parts of our own land as well [as] from
foreign countries–fit tribute to him whose nobleness calls
forth universal admiration & love. How much I wished to
stop long enough to see what our country has done here–
but, the glimpses we gained in passing were all we could
now get. The pleasure of full enjoyment was reserved, in
the future which hope always promises. Our next change
was to a quiet slow boat–to go 50 miles on the Potomac.
It was an inexpressible relief–after so long a car ride with
the jarring motion so tiresome. All hurrying was over, we
were at rest on the gently moving water–scarcely moving.
Along the banks everything was as still as if sleeping the
last long sleep. With nothing striking save the stillness, it
was a beautiful picture. From the sheet of silver were reflected
every shrub, the leaves were just beginning to turn– a few
of the more tender trees had put on their robes of scarlet,
but nearly all were yet in their summer green. The little
sloops lying along the banks had every rope & even their
sable crews thrown back each apparently having a mate
looking up from the mirror below him. Miss Smith & I
were taking all the quiet loveliness of the early morning
landscape into our memories, standing on the deck, when
the breakfast bell rang, to change our source of pleasure.
Unspiritual earthly mortals we were, but, even the scene

before us could not beguile us into forgetting that we had
eaten nothing since leaving New York, & we descended to
the ladies cabin. While there we passed Mt. Vernon, the
usual signal of ringing the bell was not given, but a passenger happened to notice the spot, & speak in time for us to
go on deck again, little could be seen, but enough to recall
the grateful recollections of him who was indeed a "Father
of his country." Sacred to every true American heart must
this spot ever be which was his home. Our traveling companion Mr. Murdock chanced to have in his valise a book
containing Webster's grand eulogy upon Washington. He
read it aloud, and it never seemed before so full of meaning, coming from the greatest man America has ever seen
in token of love for her purest and truest patriot. If "the
times which try men's souls" shall come again to our land,
shall we find men who will follow his noble self-denying
example? I was glad to pass the first Sabbath morning of
my journey here—if I must travel at all then—all efforts to
postpone starting until Monday morning had been unsuccessful. We were done with crowds, with bustle & confusion—nothing now reminded one of an active every-day
working world—going ahead continually. There seems to
be a spell of repose over everything, & how could one help
falling into the same mood, forgetting that a life of earnest
real work is our destined end & way. I was leaving a sad
gloomy sorrow marked past—going to an untried future, &
could only "let the dead past bury its dead," hoping for a
brighter future, of contented usefulness at least. The morning soon passed away—at Acquia Creek we took the cars
again for Richmond & Petersburg.² We soon found warmer
weather—dusty too, & through a miserable sandy country
our route lay. Richmond was our first stopping place—an
apology for a dinner was soon dispatched & we were off
again—the country to Petersburg had some variety of scenery—at least to us the plantations were new—worn out as
they looked. It was the holiday of the week & bright ban-
dannas seemed to be displayed in rivalry with gay vests at
every stopping place. The fences were mounted by smaller
woolly heads—with every shade of complexion in their

faces, all pictures of happiness, looking as though not a thought or care ever disturbed the even tenor of their way —either with large or small specimens. Undoubtedly we were favored with a sight of some members of the wonderful world renowned FFVs—but we ignorant strangers, could not distinguish them from the common herd, a mistake which is said to be possible even among their paler owners—that is for Yankees to make.[3] Their numbers surprised me, for the old worn out look of all the land gives one an idea that it will poorly repay cultivation. The scenery was varied by intermingling of corn-fields, with the harvest all gathered & tied in bundles, & large tobacco fields—the two indispensables of life here. Without the least incident or variety of any kind, we rolled along until within a half mile of Weldon, N. Carolina, when suddenly with a tremendous jerk we stopped —every gentleman jumped to the doors & windows & the ladies of course did their share of being well scared—though no one screamed— mirabile dictum. The pleasing fact was soon revealed that engine & tender were off the track—having run over 4 mules which were sleeping too soundly to "look out for the engine when the bell rang." Three were dead—the fourth nearly so—the wonder was that many of us had not shared the same fate, our slow pace had been the only preventive of a terrible accident. The passengers soon walked to the end of the road—dêpot it could not be called. It was a Southern hotel—one story high—with a piazza all around —wheron were sundry benches—with tin basins of water & towels limpy & damp—here was our dressing room—for ladies as well as gentlemen—remembering the maxim, "when you are in Rome &tc" we soon were busily engaged removing the day's deposits of dust. My companion & I were lucky in getting the first use of the said basins, as we saw others waiting in vain for fresh water, & at last accept second-hand accommodations. We soon heard in a stentorian voice, "gennemen, de supper is ready right off," & saw by the rush that no time was to lose. In a small room swarming with flies, lighted by tallow candles, were several tables behind which stood numerous waiters with vacant staring faces – but ready to help us to the small variety there was. We had but a half-hour before we were off again for the night. It was a miserable road – poor cars & full at that. We were all glad enough to stop in Wilmington on Monday morning – though the best hotel we could find was intolerably dirty, we did not regret being obliged to wait until evening for the next train South. We ploughed through some sandy streets, found nothing of interest to see. One might easily imagine that the whole town had departed this life, & awaited a resurrection – for it was all motionless. The negroes looked old, the mules dragged their carts creaking along, just stirring. An inquisitive "live Yankee" gave us no rest in asking questions at every opportunity through the whole day. It was "tedious and tasteless" – not his questions but all around us. Hot sand to walk in outside, a close indefinite odor of all the dinners served up during the past summer pervaded the whole house. Sleep was out of the question – there were too many permanent occupants of all the beds. So we talked of home, wrote a little, & tried the universal relief for woman's ennui, crochet work. Musquitoes swarmed around us by myriads it appeared to us – but, the day passed – we left Wilmington joyfully to its repose. The stars were out when we went on board the ferry boat to cross the Cape Fear river – that was still, too, & every bright star lay on its bosom until we started them into the wildest of dances – like crazy spirits. In five minutes we were where we heard "cars is ready, gennemen" – off again for a night's ride. They were sufficiently comfortable to sundry owners of blankets & over-coats around us – if not [one] might judge by their snoring – we too soon followed their example – snoring of course excepted. My first sensations were when we were roused at two next morning to get ready for crossing the river. A novel scene it was as we went slowly down to the bank of the Great Pedee – through deep sand. The moon was up, but a heavy fog cold & cheerless hung over the water. Bonaparte used to speak of a three o'clock in the morning courage for soldiers – about the same amount is wanted for travelers it seems to me. Every-body rubbing eyes – shiver-

ing, stamping,–& so we crowded on a little flat boat–to
wait until our baggage & a heavy mail were brought down
–on the backs of negroes–who seem principled against
going out of a walk anywhere. They carried torches of fat
pine–the gas light of this region. Their shiny black faces
loomed up from the grey surroundings, we could but be
reminded of Charon & the Styx, when as the last trunks &
logs were deposited on the boat along-side of ours, we
were pushed off & pulled across by a stout man who drew
the boat by ropes fastened on each side of the river–a
specimen I suppose of Southern engineering. It was slow
work, compared with what we were familiar with as ferries,
but, we were going to a new country of course to see new
institutions–we knew there was at least one, a "peculiar institution"–On the other side was a longer waiting–for all
the baggage must be "toted" up again. We were the last
passengers favored thus–next trip they crossed on the fine
new bridge. So, we had a last chance to get a glimpse of
"jolly flat-boat men's life["]–On the cars once more for
Augusta–going through long swampy districts–now &
then passing a clearing which was always a cotton plantation. At daylight we began to see the companies of men,
women & children going into the fields with their baskets.
The fields were literally white for the harvest–beautifully
they looked with ripe pods & blossoms on the same stalks.
We were fairly in the dominions of the great "king Cotton." The appearance of all the plantations was [as] if belonging to one man–a frame house–on each side of which
were log cabins, looking as though in the midst of a flower
garden. As we passed on, I could hear from our fellow passengers comments like "that's a likely gang's nigger." "I'd
like to own about a hundred like those fellers"–"There's a
sorry crop–he must have been a poor overseer" &tc then
a general discussion of crops in different parts of the South
until the announcement of "brekfus" was made. We stopped
at a log house–in the woods–found the most uninviting
looking mixture of ham, eggs, chicken & corn bread–all
but the bread swimming in gravy. Its being our only chance
for a mouthful until we reached Augusta we were told,

made us overlook appearances of food as well as waiters
who evidently had been working in the field. As the time
for arrival is uncertain, everything apparently had been
ready & waiting no little time. Fifteen minutes more & we
were moving on–with no change of scene till we saw Augusta. Hamburg is connected with it by a fine bridge–It
was the yellow-fever season–desolation was our only impression of this beautiful city. Scarcely a man was to be
seen. We rode down the principal street, with its rows of
shops & stores closed. It has trees on each side & a third
row of them through the centre. We were expressly assured
that but a few minutes stay would be made, but it was
lengthened into two hours, made more gloomy by the in-
coherent talk of a tall, gaunt old black woman, who as was
told us by one of our number, during the prevalence of the
fever years before, spent all her time in nursing the sick.
Afterwards, several benevolent gentlemen made up a purse
sufficient to buy her & set her free, but, her mind soon
lost its balance & she has been ever since a harmless luna-
tic. She talked of fever, & volitioners (abolitionists) constantly. Unfortunately, I became the object of her special
attention & admiration because she said, "I sees de reel old
South Caliny [Carolina] blood in my young mistris' eyes"
The Cape Cod blood was to her invisible.[4] In parting she
insisted on kissing my hands. Her image will always rise up
before me when I think of Augusta. She seemed so fitting
a spirit to stalk about at such a time. With a deep sense of
relief we heard the first sounds from the engine, & still
greater was it to hear "all aboard," there were no "longing
lingering looks" were cast behind as we left. At the dinner
house about twenty of us were contentedly sitting at table,
when "de cars is done started" was the welcome news. We
followed suit, but were too late, for a few minutes we supposed nothing would stop their forward march–but soon
they approached us, & with a hearty laugh all round we re-
sumed our old seats, glad that so easily we had escaped one
of the most woeful experiences, being left behind which is
nowhere pleasant, least of all in a log-cabin on a clearing in
a Georgia swamp. We jogged along through that entire

night, through the same kind of country–slept when we
could, did the same next day until four p.m.– when we
reached Montgomery without having seen a town worth
remembering or even a village. It was warm & dusty for
the last 40 miles. What a comfort to us was the discovery
at the hotel that water was plenty–the greatest of all luxuries in such a journey. We bathed & walked for rest–found
the two lively Frenchmen again as we entered the parlor, as
full of fun & politeness as ever. Here was our last experience of cars. Mr. M. said but too truly–"after this girls,
you'll find nothing goes by steam"–Montgomery as the
geographies say "is the capitol & contains the State House
with other fine public buildings." From the steps of the
state house we gained a fine view of the surrounding country, but had no time for long walks. Dinner was to be attended to, & in fine style too was it serve[d]–the silver
was marked Lafarge, having been in that house in N. York
–with the present landlord. We were to start now for an
old-fashioned stage-ride of 150 miles–instead of the shrill
whistle & the warning bell, we heard a bona-fide stage
horn–which we all supposed was a signal for starting, but
an hour's waiting seemed not to be considered as the least
consequence. It was sunset before we were all packed in–
thermometer at 95° on the hotel piazza, "an uncommon
warm spell" they told us & we fully acquiesced, nine passengers were put inside, six on the top with baggage to
match–With Miss Smith & myself on the back seat was a
most uneasy, sharp-elbowed Mrs. Smith, whose Mr. S. was
outside thereby causing continual movings to facilitate
conversation.⁵ Fussing & fidgeting continually she seemed
bent on being miserable & making others so. She was starting, we nearly at the end of a long tiresome journey &
there is a vast difference in one's feelings. About midnight,
we suddenly stopped in the thick woods–the driver no-
ticed that the telegraph wire was down, & concluded to go
on & see why it was so, but a few rods ahead of us a large
tree had fallen directly across the road. Had our six lively
horses first made the discovery, the gentlemen said our ride
might have soon ended in the other world. The four ladies

of our company decided to walk on while the tree was being moved. The moon was giving us light enough to see the way, & we were assured there was no danger. We were enjoying it wonderfully when a strange sound filled the air—as if goblins on their nightly errands were politely accosting us with "who are you, who are you"—then would come a hollow imitation of a laugh from the dark mysterious company—The two Yankees halted suddenly—but, our company had one "old settler" who soon dispelled all our foolish fears, & I suppose the wonted color returned to our blanched cheeks—though we couldn't see it. She was in fact one of the natives—to the manner born, & just said, "Lu, me, don't you know them is nothing on with but screech owls. They eats nothing but chickens—so you needn't be a grain feard," & we left them hooting & screeching away perhaps with double gusto since they had so needlessly scared two green Yankee girls, they rolled their knowing eyes undisturbed. It seemed a trysting place for numerous kindred spirits, as we walked on—It was a lonesome sound at best, & we were like John Gilpin "right glad to hear the lumbering of the wheels again["]⁶—It was a long weary night—the consciousness of slow progress made it doubly so—though we were too much worn-out to enjoy any kind of traveling without one night's rest, from Saturday until Thursday. Morning's first grey light revealed a dismal looking unwashed unkempt crowd. A Methodist minister & idiot son—a brown-faced backwoods man with his wife who had so enlightened us on Natural History—with their hopeful—all dressed in homespun, the fit of which gave an impression of ample room for growth —copperas color en masse—Mr. Murdock & nephew, & the loving Mrs. Smith between Miss Smith & myself. A level "piney woods" country, with sandy roads is the least interesting of all prospects—swamps have luxuriance & greenness to beautify them, but a dead level of low pines & sand has nothing. Our only amusement was the conversation of the jovial minister with our party, & occasional remarks dropped by him of the copperas suit, & his consort. She relieved the tedium of the way by almost constant dipping snuff—in comparison to which the three tobacco chewers seemed models of elegance in manners. That is a practice certainly which, "to be hated needs but to be seen." We learned that "crops was sorry in their parts this year—but niggers was a'risin in price" for "likely" hands, & other kindred items. One remark of the minister to Mr. M. made a strong impression on my mind—as a solution of what he considered the mystery of such want of progress. "After all," he said we do live just this way—"We buy more land to make more cotton, to buy more niggers, to buy more &c." He was a large planter, though a preacher, & of course owned a large number of slaves. We heard some most amusing delineations of things in general, in the times of Miss. land speculation, both he and Mr. M. telling their personal exploits, when city lots were sold by the foot in places where the trees here only "blazed" to mark where streets were to be.—We came to a "post oak country["] —towards night. Selma was the only place of any size we saw—there first we found an Artesian well—it seemed like a gift directly sent from heaven—to see the pure clean water gushing out, & know that it stops not nor lessens in cold or heat, wet weather or dry. The "stands" for eating were of the poorest description—poor people & poorer fare. The chickens one would say must have died from starvation so pitiably sharp did their bones rise up from the sea of grease in which they were swimming—The poor flies even seemed to be bent on getting their accustomed fare—if we might judge by the number which had lost their lives in the rash attempt. Growing warmer as we went on, & of course more tired, the day dragged slowly away—One by one our fellow-passengers bade us good-bye until the five who started together were all the stage load. We had stopped only the time in Wilmington a few hours, & two in Montgomery since Saturday at 5 P.M. It was two P.M. on the succeeding Friday when we reached our destined end. Columbus as we first saw it, was a pretty place—but had but a week before been very much injured in the principal business streets by a large fire.[7] We went at once to the Institute for Young Ladies. Were met by a lady with a cool dig-

35

nified "how'd'ye young ladies, we've been looking for you
several days."[8] A servant was soon called to show us our
room–O, the loneliness of that great half-furnished place,
it overpowered us both. Miss S. who had just left school
& for the first time tried a life among strangers–far from
home–I who had no home felt–both of us utterly heart-
sick–& took the usual woman's way of making things better–sat down & cried–but–the first sight of each other's
faces produced a sudden change–for, there were furrows
down our cheeks–which revealed our crying need of water
–so we concluded to commence removing deposits. We
passed through a yard full of roses & other flowers, so
there was some brightness. We were tired out, & after a
short conversation down stairs, went to rest. The last
sound I heard was a drawling–humdrum of "Do they miss
me at Home do they miss me"–coming from one of the
practising rooms. We soon discovered that our lives had
fallen among the aristocracy somewhat dilapidated though
it was. We had the honor of being under the roof of a
South Carolinian who was brother to an ex-governor, &
whose wife was sister of Hon. Waddy Thompson, once
minister to Mexico–now the heads of a Female Institute–
with two grown daughters full of that double-refined gen-
tility, which like the dying dolphin shows its colors most
in its last struggles.[9] We were little skilled in worldly wisdom, but a few days taught us plainly that between us as
assistants & the family as principals a great gulf was fixed.

Nov. 18th Six weeks have gone–we are a little wonted to the
strange ways in our new home–To me the wonderful beauty
& profusion of flowers have been constant sources of joy. I
have almost forgotten the want of other things, in the enjoyment of cape jessomines & roses. Now they are fading.
It is almost December. The flowers I love so much will
soon be gone–Thus far they have been all the sweetness in
my new & uncongenial sphere of duty–I see little of the
effect of slavery–in fact, nothing except the every-day life
of servants–All we have heard of its horrors may be true–
they seem a happy, careless thoughtless race–Soon I shall

have the company of my dear & only sister—to whom I
hope this mild balmy air may prove a gentle invigorator, &
save her from our terrible family scourge—consumption—[10]

1854 Christmas. It has been to me a happy day—My dear Martha is here after the long journey arrived safely this morning—Though her home here has few of the comforts of
home at the North, we are happy in being together—We
have taken a long walk this afternoon—The roses are not all
gone yet—though the frost has taken the leaves from most
of the trees—the grand magnolias in their glosy greenness
look far more beautiful as they stand almost unrivaled. It is
a land where all have the means of happiness God sends—
all who are free to use them at least—We can see the outside world to find exhaustless sources of pleasure in it.
Time only will show us what is beyond—in the social
world. The hum-drum life of a teacher gives little variety
save what one's own thoughts afford. I think as my journey
has been noted down, for the first time in my life, I will
keep a sort of journal, perhaps not [to] be seen once in
three months, but when I feel like scribbling it may help to
while away time, perhaps now & then something may happen which I will like to look over in after years —my sister
& I together. We can jot down in short hand & enlarge at
our leisure. As another has said, "it may string the pearls
that, otherwise lying loose, might be trodden upon & swept
away."—If there are no pearls to string in our lives, "it will
recall events & feelings which might else be forgotten."

Feb. 8th / 55 The first illustration we have had of the peculiari-
ties in the vaunted "peculiar institution of the South.["]
Last night a little before twelve, I heard the gruff, harsh
voice of the South Carolina master here, calling for a cow-
hide in tones so loud that although it came up two flights
of stairs every word was distinct—Then the voice of our
maid-of-all-work Milly—repeating, "Master—I haven't got
the money—I doesn't know where it is—Master don't whip
me"—I shut my door, but, could not keep out the sound.
The awful oaths mingled strangely with her prayers—down

in the basement—then the blows came with sticks—such shrieks & sobs—until I heard "mistress" go down & beg him to stop—for Milly would be hurt—& the noises ceased —She was a light mulatto fifteen years old but a mother—I had heard gentlemen in the parlor under our room till a few minutes before, which accounted for the choice of such an hour—Today—it has been explained to me by Mrs. Means.—She prefaced by saying—I suppose you heard the noise Milly made last night, as you are not used to such things—then told me why her husband was obliged to do it—One of the young ladies boarding here has lost $20 within a few days—most naturally, Milly being chamber-maid is supposed to have taken it—She obstinately refused to confess her guilt—& then the only resort was—correction as she calls it—& so the matter stood till Madam happened to think that a friend of the robbed young lady had that day brought to her a new $10 New Orleans bill—just like those which were left & of which there were 5 alike. She told her husband that might be some clue to it, & so he stopped his correction, though I had heard him over & over in his rage say he would whip her till the money was brought—Those sounds still echoed in my ears, like nothing I ever heard before, long after every-thing was still. How I longed to speak, as I heard the story—but knew too well it would not do. I saw her this morning, creeping up the stairs, with her neck arms & face striped with marks of the stick—she was unable to walk straight—because as she said her back hurt—

Two days now have gone & the mystery is all cleared up. The young lady of 17 did the deed for which Milly was so unmercifully punished. While in charge of her friend's keys, she took $20 out, & gave away 10—the money brought to Mrs. M. On searching her trunk sundry & various other missing articles have come to light—but, she is the daughter of a rich planter, this is an uncontrollable propensity— & so our Principal says it must be "hushed up."—Many a day will come & go ere those sounds will pass from my memory—It is my first experience in the workings of slavery—I hope it will have no second—The brightest suns or fairest flowers that ever made beautiful any favored land, could not make me forget the dark shadow of cruelty at any time possible—when passions are roused—Poor innocent simple-hearted Milly could only beg for mercy—

April 5th / 55 First Sight of a Runaway
A beautiful spring morning, our first experience of the almost magical change which in a few days comes over the face of Nature. The freshness of every-thing had lured my sister & myself on till we were two miles in the country. The flowers were coming forth all around us, we had our hands full, & were just talking of the glorious beauty of such a country when we hardly realized that Winter had come before it was gone. Just as we turned to go back, we saw coming on a cross road a man on horseback riding at a quick pace, & by his side a tall negro coming steadily along. We wondered at the perfect uniformity of his steps—until, as they came nearer us, we saw one chain going from his wrists to the saddle, another was around his ancles—giving him just room enough to walk—Following them were two large thick-headed fierce-looking dogs.—The clothes of the negro were badly torn, too. They were gone in a shorter time than one could tell it—but, how changed seemed all the sweet things around us, for over them all was thrown the shine of that serpent slavery. We had read of slaves being chained & supposed it only the exaggerated fancy of over-zealous fanatics. Here was the unvarnished truth, with no need of fancy's touch to make its horrors more vivid, no room to imagine it worse than the stern reality. The captor was as we were afterwards told a "nigger hunter" by profession—by the side of whom his dogs looked like a far superior race of beings—for they were all their Maker gave them power to be—he a beast with power to be a man.

May 1st. We have heard the mockingbird high up among the branches of an old pine, he was filling the air with melody which might have inspired a poet as did the skylark when poor Shelley wrote his exquisite "Hail to thee blithe spirit"[11]

—None other than a true poet could describe the countless variations of sweet sounds which this plain little Quaker looking singer pours forth. We sat in silence for a half hour on an old log—out of sight—there was or seemed to be no repetition, no stopping for breath, he was practicing alone, his part in the grand oratorio of creation this beautiful spring. To us it seemed like midsummer, the roses were beginning to grow pale & the heat was oppressive. One could imagine nothing but joy in the world of which he seemed to be telling—it was far above us—as he was out of sight—so we could but think is that purer life which "eye hath not seen, nor ear heard, neither hath it entered into the heart of men to concieve." Sweet sounds like these always come like faint echoes from the harmonies of heaven—enough to tell us of a music which will never die away. Away in a piece of woods we heard an answering voice catching up his strains so faintly at first that we scarcely heard it. Was it his answering spirit—like the spirits made perfect alone—do they answer to our earthly calls—for companionship in hours of loneliness—whispering gently to our dull ears of their present home, & telling us that the highest purest joys we can know here, are but poor foreshadowings of the hereafter—

New Year's Day / 56 "Hiring Out"

By invitation of a friend I went this morning to his plantation twelve miles in the country—my first insight into plantation life.[12] When about half way there we saw quite a large crowd assembled on the "porch" and scattered about the yard of a double log house. My friend at once understood that there was to be a negro hiring & asked if I would like to see it. I assented & we rode up to the door. With but one exception, every man was dressed in copperas colored home made jeans. Mr. C., my companion, at once became an Esq. by virtue of his black suit. I was escorted into "the room" where was a man making out bonds for those hired. I read one, which obligated the person named to pay the sum of 120 dollars for Rose & two small children, payment to be made monthly for the ensuing year to her master or his agent, and moreover she was to be furnished a change of clothing, two blankets & suitable food. The lady of the house gave me all necessary information unasked. The "niggers" to be hired were she said the property of some orflins [orphans] for whom her husband stood 'guardian.' I sat by an open window & the business soon began. A large block was brought & placed on the highest spot. Around it gathered the crowd of tobacco chewers, now & then I saw a black bottle passed round among them, their voices soon telling of its virtues. The property of the orflins stood in the background dressed in their best clothes, of all colors & sizes—in fact this was true of themselves as well as their clothes. There were about 35 in all varying from the real unmistakable Africans to the pale blue eyed mulatto. My hostess commented on the subject in general, telling me "nobody but them that has it knows what a heap o'trouble orflins is to a body. Niggers never is satisfied, one of em came home last week all tore an bit by the dogs, but I didn't blame him so much for runnin off for they tied him to 4 pieces of wood made like a cross an whipped him a'most to death. He jest could git home 15 miles, an he's too badly off to be hired out to-day so we've got him on our hands like as not all the year. Then last month we had a woman to come home, she'd bin in the woods risin o' two months, an was nigh to bein perished. The overseer couldn't bring her to terms, an so undertook to whip her an she run off—we put her in jail for him to come after her, but he never came. That yeller one there is the one, you'll hear her called Suey when they put her up. Last year one o' the best men a carpenter, wouldn't work, an they made him build a coffin, then made him git into it, and nailed it up to scare him—he was a'most white, a mighty smart feller, could read an write, they said, an so they was afraid to whip him—fear he'd pay back some way. Well, they kep Jack in a leetle too long, for when they come to knock on the lid, he didn't speak, an when they opened it, he'd just done breathin—He was Suey's husband. We've tried an tried to git a judgment gainst the master but we can't he's got some rich kin-folks that always keeps him up, an the children will have to lose it I'm afeerd. He an Suey was hired to different places 10 miles apart an he would run away every two or three months to see her—when he died she went a'most crazy.["] For a half hour she had talked on these precise words I answering not one word—I could not doubt the horrid truths she told and never can I forget them, or that scene. The auctioneer's loud voice rang out, "genmen, it's a'most time to begin, it's time to bring em on." The first one was a gray-headed old man who with difficulty got up—"What'll you give me for old Jo," the bloated seller screamed out, "not much I know master,["] Jo said, ["]my work is a'most done." "Well, he'll do for hog tender—10 dollars—15—15 gone to Mr. Hankins for 15 dollars—" Next came old Joe's wife more infirm but younger than he—she went to another man just to mind the black children for a home. Then their children—Ned stepped up—"about 25, likely field hand, can do most anything—some one starts 50, 50 is bid, 60—65—65 worth double genmen, 75—80—100— 125 then up to 150—cheap at that—gone to Charles Slocum for 150." He stepped down and went to his new master, then came a large girl & two smaller children, "only large enough for cotton pickers"—They were soon bid off, and their places were filled by others—who went lively as the current expression was, as cotton was likely to be high & "hands scarce." About a dozen were disposed of, when there came a tall slender, well-formed light mulatto woman with two children about 7 & 9 yrs. old, and a baby in her arms. "Here's Suey, got no husband to bother her, what'll you give—want the children to go along if we can—50—75 —85—100—without the children." Here the woman fixed her black eyes on the man bidding. Mrs. H. told me twas "a rich old bachelor, mighty rich from cross the river, but hard on niggers"—Some one kept running against him until it went up to 150—175—& she was "struck off" to the rich man—She said not a word, but her looks told what was in her heart, as she gave up the two older children, she sobbed bitterly—Any other expression of feeling would I suppose have been punished—Here was one of my own sex almost as light in color—with a poor shabby dress of mourning for her husband still on her. I could not keep back my own tears, though they were unobserved by others. Suey's place was next filled by a young, fine-looking gaily dressed "house girl" who went to "the Squire" of that county. Some looked happy—knowing their masters—they could calculate so far as eating & drinking went with tolerable certainty & this to them makes up the sum of life. While the bonds were being settled one & another related instances of violations of them & injuries by whipping which all agreed—"the laws orter take in hand." One in the neighborhood was paralyzed for life, perfectly helpless from too much whipping, another woman had started twice to drown herself, & "was well whipped for it too"—I heard an animated discussion on the use of dogs in catching them— it was denounced—because so often hands were laid up after it and couldn't work. It was new strange talk to me— indescribably revolting—How from my inmost soul I detested those creatures in the form of men who could thus calmly in a perfect matter-of-fact way discuss subjects which to me seemed only fit converse for fiends. We spent perhaps two hours there—it seemed to me but a glimpse of the lower world & its foul deeds—and yet it is done at the beginning of every year all over the "Sunny South"—How thankful was I when we rode away from the sight of so much helpless hopeless misery, which I was powerless to relieve—

After six miles farther ride we came to the plantation which to me possessed but one interesting feature, a family of Albinos—with genuine negro features but hair almost white & very curly, eyes of a pinkish hue without the power of contraction & dilation in the pupils so that in bright sunlight they could see very little, they are of little use as "field hands" I was told. The mother was black, her husband a mulatto—three of her children were albino—two were black. One of them a boy about 12 showed a wonderful mathematical talent, answering every question his master asked him even to large sums in multiplication—he had never been taught even the simplest principles in the use of figures–Their appearance is extremely repulsive, always winking.

July 10th / 56 An entirely new view of the "peculiar institution" has been shown us today–The seamstress of the house, Anne a bright mulatto of about forty, brought me this morning a letter from her mistress Miss Nash of N. Carolina. Anne's story was this–her husband to whom she had been married 20 years was sold for his master's debts & sent to Miss. They belonging to different persons, after some years Anne heard from him, & being a favorite servant got permission to accompany a gentleman & wife as nurse for their child in coming here. She has been here six months with John, sending back her wages every month in the meantime. I have written several letters for her to her mistress at home. Now the news is, her old master is dead – her mistress writes, "Nearly everything must be sold to pay old debts.["] She was told to make her choice to be sold where she would be with her husband, or come back & share their poverty at home–"You have always been a faithful servant Anne," wrote her mistress–"we can no longer live as we have done, your Miss Maria & I will have to teach to support ourselves–don't think we will be offended if you wish to stay with John. You must ask God to help you in deciding right, remember after-wards, I can do nothing more for you. If you wish to stay there, find a good master & I will sell you for $1000 dollars in cash. Write soon to your friend & mistress–H. Nash." She was overcome with grief at her master's death, & the sad state of affairs at home. In her own words, "it's too much for my master Judge Nash's wife to come down so, an his daughters raised so like ladies, now they're gettin' old, have to work. We've all played so much together, Miss Maria an I is jest one age." Then she would talk of John who she said was always good to her, and she couldn't tell what to do. He belonged to a carpenter that being his own trade. She could not think of being the servant of any one but a gentleman–as she said, "I never been used to no other sort-o-people, an I couldn't live with them." She wanted me to tell her of any of my friends who would be likely to want her where she would have a good house—"any one you like would be good to me" was her simple reasoning. It was new business—opened a new train of thought & feeling. The necessity in her case was plain—there was no alternative—in it I had no responsibility—I sent her to a friend Mr. J. Hamilton, who in talking with her found that her master & his father were old friends.[13] He writes back to Miss Nash he will take her sending the money in any way she chooses. He told Anne to ask me to read his letter, and add what I knew of his wife, which I have done. I have little doubt that when a return mail comes from N. Carolina, Anne who says she is the child of one of the richest men there, will be the property of a son of Alexander Hamilton here.

Christmas week, 1856. The long, sultry summer has passed away, taking with it all feeling of energy. Vacation was spent in nursing dear Martha through an acclimating fever, for amusement I tried an experiment in the way of chills for three months, but, for the present at least, have given up the attempt as unsuccessful in its results. A short trip to Mobile broke the spell which deafening doses of quinine often repeated had failed in doing. The city possesses little attraction except in the line of fish & oysters which were a great luxury to a native of Cape Cod, who hadn't tasted anything in about two years so suggestive of one's native soil—the ocean. The grand magnolias all along the banks of the Tombigbee, & larger ones still about Mobile are most beautiful features in the level landscapes. The city has still some old residences of the Spanish aristocracy who first settled it, old, but venerable, for therein lived "the first families"—Had the pleasure of seeing the famous Madame Le Vert, one of the "crème de la crème" of Southern society—Was offered the honor of an introduction, but declined as I knew the acquaintance of a "Yankee teacher" would be no acquisition to her, and I have no tact for saying "taking" things to strangers—In Mobile I formed some idea of the amount of cotton shipped from there, by going to the wharf where lay immense piles of bales, each with a flag on its top, marked to distinguish each merchant's lot.

Small "lighters" were being loaded as fast as the swarms of negroes could tumble over the bales, to carry them down over the bar where larger vessels lie in waiting. Though an uncrowned one, in some senses certainly "Cotton is king.["] There is no other monarch in this latitude at least.—Having one object, intent on gain in only one way—so far the remarks of the Methodist Rev, our fellow passenger in the stage, has been confirmed by all my observations, "We buy more land, to make more cotton, to buy more niggers"— One used to the wide-awake life in the North gets tired of a dead-level monotony. Save now & then a murder, or a duel which seconds half the time settle without a shot being fired—the stagnant waters of social life are seldom rippled by any excitement. A part of the programme in every wealthy planter's family is the annual Hegira "North" —then wait for the next year's crop to grow, while the "hands make it"—and, unless they make far more than can be gathered with a long face Mr. Planter will tell you he had a "mighty sorry crop"—also, the rains never come just in the right time & quantity to suit—a peculiarity not confined to this latitude. Verily—"Our content is our best having."

January 10th / 57—How lonely it is tonight. Martha has gone to teach in the lower part of the State—I miss her everywhere —While she was here I never felt all alone, now it seems written on everything—The spring which moved me forward is gone, & I can only think over & over for what am I living, to whose happiness am I contributing. The dull round of daily duties in teaching is I hope faithfully gone through, but how little of my real self goes into that. It is merely machine work, fast becoming intolerably irksome— & just for dollars & cents. How long it is since I have heard a new thought expressed, or seen a strange winning face. Now & then, thank Heaven a fresh book finds its way to us, & what invitation goes nearer to the heart than

> "Come and take choice of all my library
> And so beguile thy sorrow"—[14]

It is next to human sympathy – & yet lacks something,

> "In all the counsel that we two have shared
> The sister's vows, the hours that we have spent."[15]

how much of happiness now is only in the past. The violets are just beginning to show their blue eyes, full of sweetness, & bearing with them the promise of many more bright flowers, which will not be long in coming – the compensation for so much one finds wanting in "The Sunny South" –

Small Pox

April 24th Nearly four lonely months have passed & today a new field of duty seems opened for me. Columbus is thoroughly roused by a case of small-pox. A poor boy son of a widow has come up from Mobile sick – the physicians pronounce it smallpox – which has electrified the town with fright.[16] This morning I met the Dr. attending who told me no one could be found who would go or send a servant to his mother's assistance. Many have gone into the country, beside themselves, they forget that there is any one in danger, & forget the poor widow's wants. An ordinance was this morning passed by the city council "imposing a fine of $50 on any person who should go to the house of Mrs. Dupree & come away from there except the attending physician" – I am in no danger from the disease – A solemn vow was made while I was suffering from it, & on what I supposed must be my death-bed, that if then my life were spared – in gratitude for all the care & kindness I then received, I would do all in my power to return it – when & whereever I could. That was in Mass – now in Miss, I have first to test my sincerity in making that resolution. *I will go.*

25th – I have tied up my bundle, a change of old clothes, for I promise to bring nothing away, and in a few minutes start for the house – Now must write Martha to assure her I am safe –

May 5th—Out of my temporary prison, for the danger is over.
Found the boy not very sick with varioloid, his mother
terribly frightened, she met me crying, & then resigned her
charge to me as I was not afraid. The Dr. lay in another
room with every symptom of the disease but the eruption.
The old negro "granny" hobbled in from the cabin in the
yard, bent nearly double with rheumatism, crying like
"Miss Sally" as she called her, "Oh missus, de mos blessed-
est ting in dis whole worl is a friend, such as you is to us
when king Jesus sent you."—And this was our household—
John the sick boy of 15—groaning all the time, half from
fright, which added to almost incessant thunder & lightning made that first night at least a sleepless one to me.
Next day the Dr. a stranger to me, was worse, & told me
all disease attacked his brain most powerfully—fear of him
in case of delirium—filled up my imagination all the second
night—but, next day his fever decreased in two days more
it was gone, & he left—the boy soon got better—friends
put through the fence what was necessary for us—even one
handsome bouquet came to me—The week was a long one,
but on Saturday the Dr. said I could leave soon. Sunday
was another stormy gloomy time. Had a chill in the morning but we spent the evening in reading the Psalms aloud—
"granny" often ejaculating "dat's so, prais de Lord" &tc.
On Monday evening I left—overpowered by the expressions
of gratitude from the poor mother, son & "granny."—It
has been a greater pleasure to have had it in my power
to give even the little I have to them than to have recieved
all I did while in like circumstances—A few words in three
separate lines not long since made a strong impression
on me—

> Do today the nearest duty—
> God gives us enough, when he gives us opportunity.
> For a dead opportunity there is no resurrection.

From whom they first came, I cannot tell, but, they have
sometime been impressed on my memory, & during the
last week have often come back to me—as I have tried to
act in their spirit—

Tuesday night 6th What shall I say in reply to the note accompanying a present of silver which today has taken me so utterly by surprise, coming from those who I supposed knew nothing of my being where I was.[17] It is a new feeling—what I thought the least I could do with a quiet conscience— seems to have looked far differently to others—I can in some degree understand why "the full soul is silent." for words seem to stop where thought begins. Tomorrow, when I feel less I may say more, at least enough to answer—

May 9th In as few words as possible, I succeeded in making a poor reply to the note—This morning, I was no less surprised than at first, as I find both writings in our paper. It may accord with popular taste here, but is very far from my own. It was too small a thing to "note abroad" on either side. I have waked this morning to find myself famous—at least "in the paper"—As it may be the last time, until it is there for other eyes than mine, I'll save the "clipping." like good old Capt. Cuttle, "when found I'll make a note of it"—Besides this event which I shall long remember, another transpired, on that day—a duel between two young men of "our first families"—cause—the sister of Mr. Moore had in a note to a mutual friend said, ["]I do not consider Dr. Vaughn a gentleman"—whereupon chivalry demands that Dr. V. call out Mr. M. to answer for what Miss Eunice gave as her opinion. Mr. Moore when challenged, although he had never seen Dr Vaughn, of course like his sister "does not consider him a gentleman" & refuses to fight—At once the second, an old schoolmate & friend of Mr. M. assumes the challenge, & sends it in his own name, in which event Mr. M. will not accept it—but then can honorably return to the Dr.—all going on in two hours time—& the place—weapons—time being fixed—next morning at five, across the Alabama line 10 miles away—the parties met—Mr. M. saying as they took positions, "I never saw Dr. Vaughn before." They stood up like gentlemen, fired like gentlemen, tried to kill each other like gentlemen—took on one side a lock of hair, on the other, a piece of coat collar.

the seconds told them, their honor was vindicated, and after shaking hands, all the crowd returned to town – towering examples of southern aristocracy – gentlemen both now and henceforth – who dares say nay –

July 4th With not one sound to remind me of the day, our nation's birthday – here I sit, weak, tired of heat, tired of my room, if I had a home on earth, how homesick I should be – nearly two months have dragged along, with no change to me – A long sickness has for the first time in my life kept me shut up, & much of the time, unable to sit up – with a cough & pain in my side – My friends tell me now, they have thought I was going, as five sisters did, with consumption – but, I never for a moment had one fear – perhaps if I had more strong ties to earth, I would dread their loosening – Save my dear brother & sister, I have little left to love & live for. I am now slowly recovering – some work is yet undone – where & what it is I know not. These weeks have been a time for thought – sad, memories have been revived, they come with almost their first bitterness – those dark years of watching & waiting for the next blow, which could so plainly be foretold, & never failed to visit us – till in 7 years father, mother, a brother & five sisters all were taken[18] – I have had left, two dearer to me than mere life, a strong faith – & constant health – power "to labor and to wait" till the silver lining of those dark clouds could once more be seen – The only brightness here, has been the untiring kindness of friends – many of them strangers before. The sweet flowers & other tokens of their sympathy for me have been dear to me feeling so alone – but, my dear Martha will soon be here. I have kept from her the true state of my health, fearing its effect on her more delicate nature. May Heaven spare us to each other.

July 15th. Yesterday another surprise came to my room. A bracelet & cake basket were sent, with this note –

The undersigned a Committee representing the Mayor & Aldermen of the Town of Columbus, are instructed to ask your acceptance of the accompanying bracelet & Cake basket

as a slight token of regard which the Board entertains for
your disinterested efforts to relieve those suffering with the
Small Pox. Far from the home of your youth, surrounded
by strangers, you nobly resolved to alleviate the suffering of
those who were not only unknown to you, but unable to
render you any return – The intrinsic value of the articles we
are aware can not be esteemed – but, we trust, the thanks
of a whole community tendered through us, will be re-
garded, to which please add the esteem & respect with
which we are personally your friends –

Levi Donnell, Mayor

Geo. R. Clayton⎫ Aldermen
Abm Murdock ⎭

16th Today I made an attempt to reply in these words.

Gentlemen, My thanks are due to this community, & to
you as its public officers for your recent expressions of kind
feeling recieved by me. The little good it has been in my
power to do, has, by your generosity, been returned a hun-
dredfold, in those words & deeds which make one who
was not long since a stranger soon cease to feel herself
such. To the friends from whom they come, I can only say,
may some kind remembrance remain with you, as long as
you may be assured it will in the heart of,

C. R. Seabury

Surely, in the last few weeks I have had many proofs that
there are warm kind hearts here, with ready sympathy –
how gratefully does my weak depressed spirit recieve them.
In health they would be pleasant. In sickness they have
been everything. For the first time I realize what is the
meaning of all we read in books about "Southern hospital-
ity" – for I have felt it in full measure – not least of all, the
unwearied kindness of a physician, who would recieve only
my thanks for his numerous visits. Here I feel the force of
the words of Bacon, "No metaphysician ever felt the defi-
ciency of language so much as the grateful." – [19]

August 4th I am cheered today by the presence of my dear sister – looking well, better than I ever saw her – God only
knows how thankful I am for I dare to hope that she will

51

outlive the danger of our family disease – I am gaining slowly in strength, hoping to be ready for work again in October.

Oct. 19th Our school has begun, & I have tried to do my accustomed work – but, cannot – something is wrong which often depresses me. It is a new sensation to breathe with difficulty, often with pain, but I must not, cannot give up to my feelings. so long as labor is possible. –

Mobile, Ala.

Christmas week – Writing has been so tiresome that I have forswarn the use of the pen for pleasure – in many months – A short trip has at least for a time broken my chills This city looks in no way changed since I saw it before – Cotton cotton everywhere – & in everybody's mouth. Great pyramids of oranges are piled in front of the stores on the river banks – wonderfully beautiful & tempting. I saw one hedge this morning filled with fruit – not eatable – but, for ornament merely. Two days more, & I turn my steps homeward.

Columbus, Jan 2nd [1858] Midnight – The blow I have feared so long has come. My last darling sister met me this morning pale, & haggard, with the unmistakeable marks which hemorrhage leaves. They all tell me it was slight – soon over. – All is over with 7 others – whose first symptoms were slight cough – slight bleeding from the lungs. – Can I give up my last sister – feel that she is slowly, surely going to join the others. – With the dark past like a spectre before me, I do not dare to hope & my only prayer is that as the days of trial come for each I may recieve the strength necessary. I must hide the grief which fills my heart, & smile when it seems breaking, work with nerveless hopeless patience. The nearest duty must be done looking no farther than today. – A pall seems settled over this New Year – under it are crushed my heart's strongest affection. I am too weak in mind & body to rise above its weight. Can I bear it – as a Christian should – through this dark night of bitter agony – "I will never leave thee nor forsake thee," says

the word of God – would that to-night they seemed spoken
to me – I have read of storm-tossed sailors in the darkness
straining their eyes to catch a glimpse of a beacon light –
when a darker cloud was gathering and of many a vessel
shattered on the pityless rocks –

June 14th 1858 –

I said six months ago the blow had come – then I only saw
its foreshadowings – Now it is all over – One week ago, I
laid her down amid the sweetest flowers to sleep her last
long sleep – Our souls by long companionship had grown
to be one – and she has gone to the home she would tell
me was only a little way off – O how far it seems from this
cold world – in it I am alone, alone. Her gentle spirit, pa-
tient under suffering – peaceful in death – all ripe for heaven,
was so early taken away – In the silent nights how I listen
for that feeble low breathing I have watched so long –
Sometimes I cannot feel that she is not here – O what utter
worthless dross must be my heart, when it needs such re-
fining fire, to purify it. What sins stain my life record that
such punishments are sent upon the offender. I sat by her
grave this evening until the twilight had faded into night –
& I longed to lie beside her in that quiet spot, to struggle
no more with overwhelming sorrows which have shadowed
my whole life – for what is the future here but a lengthened
suffering – I know that she is happy – but I cannot miss her
less – there is a vacant spot no matter where I turn – nothing
left to love or care for here – nothing but a constant hollow
questioning with myself – why was she taken from my heart
– The dark river of death has washed away my memories of
our sweet conversings – all is dark to me. It is all pure self-
ishness – to grieve for her, but, O, how everywhere,

> "I miss that bright blue eye,
> That shut, and left a spot of night in all
> The places where we used to be." –

I found her grave covered with fresh flowers which she so
much loved. How often she spoke of the flowers which
will never fade away – in heaven – Now, that she is not here,

they seem to have lost half their sweetness to me. How can
I live without her.

June 15th – I have today recieved a touching work of sympathy –
delicately expressed – I know not what to say – "The poor
common words of courtesy Seem such a very mockery." –
The only spot on earth I can call my own, that in which lies
her precious body – is given me – by those almost strangers
– by this deed –

> "For and in consideration of the benevolent exertions
> of Miss Caroline R. Seabury in the cause of Human Suffer-
> ing – The Trustees of Friendship Cemetery belonging to
> Covenant Lodge No. 20 Mc Kendree Lodge No. 23 and
> Tombigby Encampment No. 6 Independent Order of Odd
> Fellows do hereby give grant and convey unto her the said
> Caroline R. Seabury, Fractional Lot numbered Thirteen
> (13) north in said cemetery And we hereby guarantee to
> her the right of burial of herself, her family or friends, and
> for no other purpose.["]

Harrison Hale ⎫
L Donnell   ⎬ Trustees
Geo. C. Brown ⎭

16th – It has been a hard task to find any words with which to
express my feelings – they leave no room for thoughts – I
have tried in this way –

Messrs –
Harrison Hale
L Donnell
Geo. C. Brown

Gentlemen –
In tender sympathy with a lonely orphan's sorrow you
have presented to me that spot where my last sister sleeps
["]that sleep which knows no waking" Her thanks are min-
gling with my own as I acknowledge your kindness, though
that voice is silent forever – You have remembered those
whom God never allowed His chosen people to forget – "the
stranger and the fatherless." though they be not within the

54

links of that chain which binds your Fraternity together. At whatever point my life-journey shall cease, earth will hold no resting-place to which my heart will turn with more earnest longing–than that shaded grave in your Friendship Cemetery.

New Years Day–1859

What new thoughts–new hopes does it bring to me–or what new duties to be done–In so monotonous a life, one can scarcely tell. I sat this evening by dear Martha's grave, only the ivy is green there now–I know it is right that she is sleeping there–safe from all trouble. I know it was,

> "Well done of God to halve our lot,
> And give her all the sweetness"–

but how I miss her everywhere–How purposeless life seems. I read, but cannot think–for my heart is too full–I work–but–feel no incentive to exertion–for it all centres and ends in myself. It is an isolation I have never before felt–It is strange that so much of grief must be sent. I can only pray that,

> "Henceforth my own desire shall be
> That He who knows me best shall choose for me,
> And so, whate'er His love sees good to send,
> I'll trust it's best, because He knows the end."

Would that I could realize the exalted truth that is expressed in the lines,

> ["]Because she bears the shell that makes the shellfish sore
> Be thankful for the grief that but exalts thee more."

April 5th / 59

Today I have been to see a part of the cargo of the *Wanderer*–a condemned slaver whose human freight was ordered by government to be sent back to Africa, but the poor Congo negroes are being smuggled into the interior states and sold in "droves" of from 6 to 12[21]–They are very delicately formed with small hands and feet. The men have their front teeth sawed off, to slant at their ends and fit ex-

actly–They will not eat cooked food, or wear clothing of
any kind–at first–now–they are somewhat changed. All
the ministers are loudly denouncing the sin of bringing
them from their native land into slavery. Yet–no one says
that constant buying & selling here is wrong in the least.
To me it seems that there is scarcely the difference–twixt
tweedledum and tweedledee–if that vexed question in
metaphysics could ever be decided–Let the sin rest on
whomsoever it may, from my inmost soul I pity them–for
they show plainly that a life of labor will be a new thing to
them–and a hard one it will be in the cotton fields here–

16th–I was not a little amused this morning in reading an advertisement of "The Sunny South["] a new paper to be published near here, at Aberdeen, "It will be free from the
"isms" of the day, in direct opposition to the spirit of all
agitators–*on purely Southern principles*["]–&tc &tc Ending
"*Our first number will be issued* as soon as we can obtain
press and paper from *the North*"–Verily, "we are the people
& wisdom will die with us."–

In the same paper were these two notices of ills that Southern flesh is heir to–and their remedies–I begin to feel that
I must see my "native land" again–As the heat increases,
my inclination keeps pace with it. to see my dear brother
once more–but I must wait till the year's duties are over in
July–

October 15th Have passed a most delightful summer–most of it
in Manchester, Vt. with uncle Edwin's family.[22] It was refreshing to see once more some mountains, something
above this dead level scenery. It recalled all my enjoyment
of the White Mountains, though these are less in height–
but when a thunder storm rolled over Mount Equinox and
spent its fury in the valley where we were, there was enough
of grandeur to make us poor mortals tremble–even though
we were enraptured with its beauty–We have walked, rode,
fished, enjoyed all the place afforded–*one* has laid up in
memory food for future hours, when the dull life of duty

RAN AWAY

FROM the subscriber, in the month of February last, a woman aged about 30, rather heavy set, short, weighs about 145 pounds, almost white, has long hair, (brown, or sandy,) blue eyes, large mouth, good teeth, and talks freely.

She claims to be free and white, calls herself EMILY RILEY, tells a wonderful tale of her father's being a flatboatman on the waters of the Tennessee. She is rather clumsy in her walk, has large feet, and had a tetter on one thumb that has injured the nail.

A liberal reward will be pa'd for her delivery to me or for her confinement in any p'ace so that I may get her. I. SULLIVAN.

Hayes Creek, Carroll Co., Miss.—4w.

This newspaper clipping concerning a runaway slave was pasted onto page 50 of Caroline Seabury's diary. Courtesy of the Minnesota Historical Society.

needs some sunshine even though it be but reflected from the past—In my rambles with Channing up the mountain sides—through the quiet meadows—how often we thought and said—our dear Martha would have loved these scenes so much—would have drunk in all their beauty, but she is seeing the glories of a land where no night comes—Now, that I am back again in the familiar places where we walked together, I miss her O, so constantly—but 'tis so hard to say even now,

"Well done of God to halve our lot,
And give her all the sweetness,"–

Jan. 1st. 1860 With nothing new to say here, I sit down because now and then, I love to talk to myself on paper—every

New Year brings with it hopes and thoughts for the future
–to the Christian it should be another starting point towards the goal, a new incentive to "closer walk with God"–
A year and half has passed since together dear Martha and
I joined ourselves to God's outward church here. She in a
few days went to the far heavenly home, all struggles over,
all sorrow past. What fruits have these months of labor
brought forth in my heart. Has the frequent consciousness
of her gentle presence been to me the spiritual strength she
used to tell me it might be. Does her love still draw my
soul away from the turmoil of earth to those calm heights
from whence she looks on me, that place which she calls
home, and we call heaven,

> "We hope, we aspire, we resolve, we trust,
> When the morning calls us to light and life,
> When our hearts grow weary, and ere the night,
> Our lives are trailing the sordid dust."

Sometimes, in the stillness of soul which deep grief leaves,
these aspirations become to us realities–life seems a glorious privilege–then some petty trial clips our wings and
we fall dejected, spiritless–As we could not always live on
mountain tops, so, I suppose we need these falls, to teach
us how little of self-sustaining power we posses–though it
be a hard lesson we must learn to "rise by things that are
under our feet," to forget our own sorrows, to seek for
some end beyond our own good. The world is full of objects to whom we can be ministers of good, if we will seek
for them.

> "The trivial round, the common task
> Will furnish all we ought to ask,
> Room to deny ourselves–the road
> That leads to glory and to God."–

It seems so much easier to yield when heavy burdens are
laid upon the heart–when God's providence leaves us no
alternatives but to "be still"–

June 1st–The first day of summer–one can hardly realize it here
–where for three months the sun has been pouring upon

us his hot breath–the flowers are withering–all save "king cotton" is languishing with the intense heat–without it in this land in vain would the sower plant his seed–so we must submit, though we be in a "melting mood"–We being to hear election talked of again–in angry tones–threatening but to me it seems like the lightning we so often see blazing in the sky–having no effect, but to show the extreme heat–followed by no showers–So long as every shoe that is worn, every yard of cloth, yes, every pin comes from the North–who can for a moment believe in the talk of disunion–The papers are beginning to hint at "dark possibilities" "threatening contingencies" which may arise &tc –if the South does not control matters and things in general when another president is nominated–As yet, all is confusion–The lost election seemed to arouse all the sleeping demons of hate towards the North, and let them loose in this land, but this promises far more bitter fruits–if words mean anything–

October 20th–Unexpectedly I have once more been to "the land of my fathers"–seen many soul-stirring sights more than I had supposed possible, have had my feelings touched in sympathy with the South–as I have heard the scathing denunciations of public speakers North, seeing "Wide Awake" processions &tc–The great one in New York by torchlight was a splendid show–If that be a type of the North generally, they are rightly named. The Charleston Convention having divided the strength of this section–only adds power to these opposers of Southern policy[23]–Having neither brains nor inclination to meddle with politics, feeling that it is no part of a woman's sphere, I have come back–loving my friends here, loving the spot where my dear Martha lies, and all the sacred associations connected with it–Not that I love or believe in the institution of Slavery–with that I have nothing to do–for it I shall never be called to account–

Nov. 15th–The question is settled–Abraham Lincoln is by an overwhelming majority elected president of the United States.–Numerous opposers here voted either for Brecken-

ridge or John Bell–but–divided, they were powerless–
Now "nous verrons."[24]

Jan 18th [1861] Commotion everywhere–notes of hurried preparation for war–It seems impossible that anything beyond
words will come of it–They have been most lavishly spent
many a time before–still there is a tone of bitter determination–a constant reiteration of the fixed purpose to prevent
Lincoln's inauguration on the 4th of March–as it could
not be prevented by ballot they say it shall be by bullets–
Who can hear even hints of war without a shudder–It is
impossible–bound together as we are–by the ties of marriage & common interests–as well as common parentage,
in numberless cases. God forbid that these strong ties shall
ruthlessly be severed–On the 20th of last December South
Carolina seceded from the Union by a vote said to be unani-
mous in her State Convention. On the 9th of this month
Mississippi followed her example–and now we are said to
be under no government[25]–Bells were rung–shouting &
tumult proclaimed everywhere that the people were trying
to make it a joyful event–It brings no such feeling to me,
it seems more like a leap in the dark flying from ills which
perhaps we have–to more dreadful ones we know not of.

Feb 16th–A company has left here today for Pensacola–to assist
in taking Fort Pickens an undertaking which many pronounce an impossibility.[26]

April 16th–The inauguration of President Lincoln is over–
without bloodshed–though it is reported by our papers
there was great fear among his friends and every precaution
used to preserve him from danger–

April 17th–The first gun has been fired, and by the South–Fort
Sumter off Charleston was attacked on the 12th of April,
& on the 14th Major Anderson in command, it was surrendered to the Confederate forces under Gen. Beauregard[27]–The telegraph announces that it has caused tremen-

dous excitement at the North—Mr. Lincoln has called for
75,000 men.

20th—Yesterday some Massachusetts troops were fired on while
passing through Baltimore on their way to Washington—I
can imagine how the cool New England blood rises to a
boiling heat as this news travels over the wires—I know too
well their spirit to believe for a minute that they will have
henceforth any other watchwords than "Conquer or die"—

June 1st The notes of "war to the knife" are sounding on every
hand—The passions of men are roused to their greatest intensity—Ambition to be a leader where the crowd follow
without one dissenting voice—urges many on. devotion to
what they think the best good of the South hurries the
masses forward—In the extracts we get from Northern papers, it is constantly reiterated that three months will "end
the rebellion"—They can understand little of the earnestness with which all women as well as men have entered
into it—

[clipping, First War Extra]

June 18th Have today recieved a long letter from uncle Edwin
urging me to leave what he regards this doomed country
full of bitterness, strong in the belief that not many months
hence this "infernal rebellion" will be crushed from the
earth—Then with the generosity his heart always prompts
he says—"come away—you shall never want for anything so
long as I live,"—It is no easy task to decide what is best to
do. I must leave strong attachments here—friends who in
my sister's & my own long sickness proved themselves true
—Her grave is here. I know there is sorrow in store for the
whole land—I am willing to do all in my power wherever
Providence shall place me to lessen that trouble—less here
in sympathy with the cause than with persons who suffer.
There I could not hear unmoved the shouts of exultation
when a great victory was gained—if those terrible battles
come which are a part of other wars. I cannot yet feel but

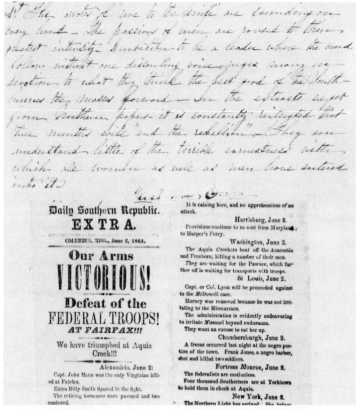

A newspaper clipping pasted into Caroline Seabury's diary describing the Confederate victory at Aquia Creek, Virginia, in June 1861. Courtesy of the Minnesota Historical Society.

that an interposing Hand will prevent much bloodshed between brothers as these two enemies are. Sometimes, it is hard "back from the lip the burning word to keep" when I hear taunts of "Yankee cowardice," the truth I know will some day flash on those who so mistake their opponents—if the full powers of each be tested—Had I a father or mother not a moment's delay would keep me from going to them—Without a home except one of dependence—I had rather work & suffer here—

July 4th – How different from any other anniversary of our national independence – To me there is sadness everywhere – a gloom over everything I cannot feel the exultation which the victory in a trifling engagement at Bethel has caused.[28] It seems but the precursor of grander events – I know defeat never conquers a determined spirit – and many a brave heart must cease to beat before such a contest is decided if once in earnest commenced. There is but one quiet spot for me – away from the tumult of this incessant quarrel – When my day's work is done – to sit by my dear Martha's last resting place – I can think of her home where "no sorrow comes – neither sighing, nor crying" and, I thank God she is spared this agony of spirit –

July 23d News has come to us that a great battle has been fought at Manassas Gap on the 21st "three days after a complete rout of Yankees at Bull's Run" which has resulted in another signal defeat of Northern forces – & fills the South with proud exultation[29] – The losses are said to be great – smaller on this side. There are many anxious hearts here waiting to know who are the killed and wounded from their own loved ones – What a call for all the heroism of the noblest woman's nature – and for all her faith in the God of battles. We surely ought to walk by faith strong and unwavering in this hour of need –

28th As the news comes home from one and another the most sickening incidents are told with perfect coolness – stories which one would involuntarily leave unfinished in reading are glibly repeated now – and this is the beginning of grim war's doings. Trophies from the battlefield begin to come back – "taken from dead Yankees" – pictures of those who were near and dear have been shown me – and I have wondered how where the same fate must befall many on both sides, it can enter any woman's heart to smile at these proofs of mortal conflict. I cannot still the questioning of my heart – could this have belonged to anyone I ever knew – Is it possible that my brother was among the number who went out – but returned no more – There are others too like

myself—whose affections are divided, who with what seems
to me hypocritical earnestness are louder in their rejoicings
than even the natives of the "Sunny South"—I cannot or
ought not to judge them—only this I feel more & more—
"Be still and know that I am God" is the voice which
seems whispering to me—then "do with thy might what
thy hand findeth to do"—These two lessons are what I ask
in prayer daily that in this trying hour—I may be able to
put in practice.

October 3d Vacation is over again, It has much of the time been
spent in working for the soldiers, for there is plenty of call
for all our time. It is hard to go to work again with everything in its present confusion—"Cui bono" will be the end
of all thought—and, there is with me a strong conviction
that we know very little of the real state of affairs either
here or at the North—The only papers now allowed being
the N.Y. Herald & Chicago Times—we see nothing of the
general feeling. More battles have been fought—victories
claimed on the Southern side nearly always—At what cost
they were gained, we know very little. Constant repetition
of promised European interference buoy up all hopes if the
scale turns at all—The most powerful blockade has closed
all Southern ports—The most gorgeous pictures which were
painted of conquest on the seas have proved thus far base-
less dreams—"King Cotton" does not yet reign—as was
predicted—Our papers begin to admit the fallacy of the old
notion—that one "Southerner is equal to six Yankees["]—In
the late engagements the result has shown them otherwise—

Feb 16th 1862—Four months more have passed away, trouble
everywhere—Now, the news of a terrible disaster to the
Southern cause. After a four days battle—Fort Donelson
which commands Nashville has been given up—with a fear-
ful loss in dead wounded and prisoners[30]—Many of our
friends were in the 14th Miss. & were taken prisoners—two
were killed, it is known—No event of the war has so come
home to us—this is the greatest conflict of the war, & has

taken some of the bravest & best–Nothing is known yet of
their destination–Our papers teem with stories of "Yankee
perfidy, sham[e]less deception, unheard of cruelty" &tc.
&tc. For the sake of my native land, most earnestly do I
hope they are exaggerated statements–for surely, such a
war needs no unnecessary barbarity to make it more like
savage conflict–

22nd–We hear today The Confederate States government is established on a permanent basis–with Jefferson Davis–
president–Alex Stephens vice pres–the great hope seems
to be failure of the finances of the North[31]–We have little
means of knowing the truth–
Whatever may betide the new government founded on this
anniversary of Washington's birthday–human foresight
cannot fathom –God help the right–

April 6th–Again we hear of the two great armies in battle at
Shiloh–but little more than 100 miles from here–Still
fighting on Sunday–"the day of battles"–"Our side completely victorious" is the last dispatch–Gens. Beauregard
& Grant commanding–The suspense is heart-rending.
Who can lie down & sleep quietly while such awful scenes
are being enacted so near us–[32]

7th–The death of Gen. A. S. Johnston is just announced and a
more guarded account of our success–To-night there are
many throbbing hearts fearing that the worst is not known–[33]

10th–The truth has come–It was ["]a retreat of the Confederate
forces–in good order"–which ended the battle of two days
–& we are told that Columbus must be the hospital sta-
tion–as it is the nearest safe point for the wounded &
sick[34]–The new hotel, our school building, the basements
of all the churches–are at once to be fitted up with cots
for the men to be brought as fast as possible on the railroad–Not a preparation has been made of either sheets,
bandages, or beds–All hearts heads and hands will be full

of work for many a day—With the energy of woman's nature when fully roused by distress—everybody is enlisted—

14th—The intense heat of today and the exciting scenes with which the town is filled—have left me exhausted—too much for sleep, but with no one to share my thoughts save my pen & paper—It is still outside—the moon has risen as calmly as though this earth were only smiling back her soft light. What far different sights we have just left—Agony in every concievable form, & even worse than positive pain, the dull apathy of hopeless sickness, when all suffering is forever past, & all hope—Crowded together in the new hotel were about 800—needing everything—with the same clothes on in which they fought more than a week ago—haggard—filthy beyond description, utterly repulsive except as suffering humanity must excite our pity, a large proportion of them with vacant expressionless faces—with wounds whose only dressing since the battle has been the blessed rains from heaven—their hollow cheeks, & glaring eyes mutely asking relief—The good face of Dr. Eve was seen here & there, he trying to bring some order out of utter confusion—From the room devoted to surgical operations came shrieks & groans, some faint as from the lips of the dying, others with the strength of intense suffering—up three flights of stairs through crowds of miserable objects—lying along the sides of the halls, we went to the fever ward—which was filled to overflowing. As none of the building had been plastered, we could see through the different rooms—and, who can ever forget it. The ladies were asked to distribute some nourishment—and how the poor wasted hands stretched out for it as we passed along—some were too weak even for that & must be fed like children, here was a mere boy, grasping a piece of bread—in the next cot, a gray-haired withered old man—with nothing but rags for clothing—his glassy eyes told too plainly that death had marked him—Not far along was a man of middle age—large frame with hands which bore the marks of hard labor, he had battled with the world in times of peace & had con-

quered—war had taken him from home, & now wasting
sickness had destroyed the strong man—His dying words
my friend could not understand. Knowing how often I
had listened for the last whisper she called me, telling him
I could hear them. He roused all the strength left & whis-
pered, "I want my body sent to my wife. I promised her—
tell her I am willing to go—my pay is due for six months—
she'll need it"—["]will you write for me & tell her this"—his
voice stopped in half an hour he was in the dead room—I
learned the address of his wife from another member of his
company—& my promise has tonight been kept—We passed
the "bunk" of one tall black eyed young man without
speaking to him—He lay perfectly quiet—but the surgeon
said there is one of the sickest men—& we turned back—
He was a lieutenant in a Louisiana cavalry company—
wasted to a skeleton but retained the marks of a true gentleman in his wan face & his manner—I had a rose in my
hand & involuntarily laid it on his pillow—he smiled—&
turned towards it. The nurse said he had been talking that
morning early about the sweet shrubs in his mother's yard
& wondering if they had come. I happened to have some
in my pocket—handed them to him. He could only say—
"thank you, I love them." I told him he should have fresh
ones everyday. When we passed his place this evening it
was vacant—he lived only six hours after we saw him—but
kept hold of the flowers the nurse said even in death—They
found quite an amount of gold about his person—he told
us—As the surgeon walked on with us—a light-haired sun-
burnt boy of about 17—raised up, & said, "Dr. don't you
know me, I'm so glad to see you"—In vain he tried to think
who the boy was—at last when told—he could hardly be
made to believe it—that the son of his old friend was there—
As we went on—he said wiping tears from his eyes —"I
have known that boy from a baby—His father is a wealthy
planter, & he an only child—what would his poor mother
say to see him now"—"I thank God no responsibility of
this war rests on my shoulders"

Just as we passed into one room—there lay one with

the sheet over his face—waiting to be carried out—His companions around were talking as though no one of their number had just left—or any of them might soon follow In one corner was one giving orders for battle—his eyes glaring wildly about—now & then he would level an imaginary gun—& exclaim—"there's one more ——— Yankee gone." He had been three days & nights thus raving—No one knew him—& he had nothing by which he could be identified, about his person In the hurried retreat companies had become divided, many had "straggled"—The poor fellow screamed to Mrs. Long—"there mother, I knew you would come & see me"—then— the most violent exertions to come to her, but his feet were tied—Some poor mother may be grieving now for him, longing for some tidings of her dear boy—and he ere long will fill a grave over which will be placed on a plain board— "Unknown"—A pretty little curly headed drummer boy looked so wishfully at us— I asked the doctor about him—He can't speak a word of English—was his reply—He is a French boy from New Orleans—I said only "avez-vous une mère" when he sprang up and commenced an autobiography at once—His mother was in France, had sent him to an uncle in N. Orleans for a business education—He had run away—was 15 yrs. old but very delicate—"Oh, mlle" ["]ma pavore mère," he would often repeat. I told him I would send him a pretty French story to read—& he would soon get better—His tears dried away soon—& he seemed quite happy as I say—bon jour je reviens une autre fois—

April 28th News just reached us that New Orleans has been taken by the Federal forces—said to have been betrayed by Gen. Lowell who was in command of the forts below.[35] Though it is a severe blow to the Southern cause, no one seems depressed by it—not a word of giving up the cause is heard. If there is half the earnestness among Northern women that there is here, we have terrible fighting yet to come. There is constant call for work, sewing, knitting, or in the hospitals The sick & wounded are every day being brought here—"Do every day the nearest duty" is all we can practise.

Diary of Caroline Seabury

[Caroline inserted into her diary the following letter from Mrs. Amanda Bush, the widow of the soldier to whom Caroline made the promise.]

May the 12 1862 mis Caroll Co

Dear madam iavaile the present Oportunity of answering
your kind and afectionate leter whitch come to hand th 11
of may iwas Glad to think that mi husband had ahope of
heaven your leter was agrate relief to me in mi distress he
said he was willing to go thank god for that Ifeele miself
under grate obligations to you for your kind Atention
towards mi husband iam more than Thankful to the pople
for thair kind Atention to him in his sickness ithank you
for Asking him questions on his dying bead it is A favior
that never will be forgoten give mi Love to the kind minister that visited him when diying ihope that he will pray for
me And mi farthless child that we may meet in heaven
Where parting none nomour it afords me grate satisfaction
ta think that we will meet again at the throne Of the lamb
ihope iwill meet you thare too It seemes that the loss of mi
husband is more than ican bare but the God of heaven has
taken him to himself ihope mi loss is his gaines In mi deep
distresse ithank you for fulfilling your promis to Mr bush
iam glad that his evrey Want was sustain ihad rather tha
the remaines Of his body had have bin sent home but as
it is Iwill have to let him lay in adistent land fare from me
Whitch distresses me very mutch but we donot no What
time may bring foruth imay be laid by his sid you said it
was apurty place and maney flours Was planted thare inever
will forgit your kindness to wards me and mi darling husband who layes silent In the tomb may god bless you ipray
icould rite severel pages it if would doaney good sowill have
ta closs ihope you will receive this leter
Mrs. Amanda bush to Miss C R seabury

May 8th Our papers are full of accounts of the brutality of "beast
Butler" as he is called in New Orleans—"his arrest of the
best citizens—daily robberies and war upon helpless women
& children"—which, if true, make his name odious beyond
the power of words to express[36]—We hear but one side—the
other might prove the maxim—"One story is good till another is told"—

June 1st The beginning of summer–how little like other years–
until the last–There is a gloom over all around–to me–
growing deeper as the months roll on–If as most say here
"God is on our side"–surely, he is causing this his chosen
people to pass through a fiery furnace of trouble. Our streets
today have been ringing with the sounds of war–one regiment leaving for Virginia–afterwards the cars brought another crowd of sick & wounded–among them are some
prisoners–I could not but look anxiously into the face of
everyone to see whether there was a familiar countenance–
captive in a strange land–When will this agony be over–
From the hour where I first saw the Confederate flag flying
to this evening there has been a conflict of feeling–personal
attachments–struggling against inborn principles–As I
heard some prisoners this evening singing Yankee Doodle,
the old familiar tune, so long unheard thrilled me with
strange emotion–I was alone, & the tears fell thick & fast–
when they in loud tones sent forth "The Star Spangled
Banner"–I cannot cease to love it. There is no little truth
in the words–"We get accustomed to mental as well as
bodily pain["] without for all that losing our sensibility to
it–& we cease to imagine a life of perfect ease as possible
for us. We are contented with our day when we are able to
bear our grief in silence–& act as if we were not suffering–
Conquerors are playing their parts on battle fields–but,
the Scripture saith "He that ruleth his own spirit is greater
than he that taketh a city"–

Waverley July 15th–For a week I have been in the quiet country
–five miles from town–where for the present I shall remain–our Vermont principal with such strong Southern
principles boiling over constantly in loyalty to the South–
having decided to employ only teachers of Southern birth[37]
–It is to me a mystery that such hollow professions do not
by their unnatural intensity produce suspicion–Let those
who can, make them. I never will–My home is pleasant,
with two little girls to teach–plenty of time for sewing,
reading, walking or riding–a great *deal too much for thinking*
–for it is impossible to fix my mind on anything discon-

nected with war, in some way. In every silent waking hour
my thoughts go to St. Paul–where nearly a year ago–I
heard for the last time of my dear brother–I cannot think
that he is fighting against this section of country–& yet
–have no means of knowing–Endless conjectures travel
through my weary brain–till I feel that almost any certainty
is better than this suspense–The lines are drawn more &
more securely to prevent any person from leaving the South
–but I feel that it will be impossible for me to stay many
months more unless I hear something–Walking ceases to
be recreation when one's mind is full of vague fears–much
as I love the country, new as are so many things to me
here, now it is unutterably lonely–and, I must be silent–

July 6th–Heard yesterday a genuine *Hard Shell Baptist sermon*–of
which I took notes on the fly leaf of an old hymn book.
The church was a log cabin in the "piney" woods–without
any but the rudest provisions for worship or comfort–It
was a convention of *foot-washers*–or those who obey literally the injunction of our Saviour "wash ye one another's
feet"–Brother Allen officiated–He was long, lank, yellow-
haired–dressed in a copperas-colored suit of home-made
cloth throughout. After a siege of coughing, spitting &tc–
he raised his head above the rough board pulpit, & began
his remarks–"Gentel*men* & ladies–I wish you to onder-
stand that this is the first time I've been into a stand sence
last fall, having ben nigh onto death–the biggest part of
the time by fur–but, I'm a'gwine ter try ter talk tell I hef
to giv it up–an then I'll quit–(here come in deep sighs, &
long spitting–with exchange of tobacco quids)–O, dear
me, I ken scasely git a breath, but I'll continner to perse-
cute on–I'm a goin to preech to you from a tex you'll find
in the leds o'this 'ere Bible, "Wharby we cry Abby Father"
–Sometimes I preeches doctrinal an sometimes expeeri-
mental discourses Now, my breethring an sisters–er–I'm
not a preechin to this ere little crowd o' hord Shell Baptists–er–but to all these ere gentlemen an ladies–er–'Bout
a year ago a brother moved into my settle*ment*–an come tu
see me–n' ses–he–'I tries tu preach sum an I onderstan yu

tries tu preech tu–now don't less hev eny trubble betwixt
us[']–Ses I tu him, ses I brother Boyd–cordin tu the ole
sayin, I don't mean tu break my shins a'stumblin over
logs–a'gitin out o' anybody's way–er I gist mean tu keep
on tu the old track–er–(Another grand cough–etc) brother
Ellis ef yu see I'm giting out o'breath, you gist stop me)–
Now gentlemen an ladies, tho' I haven't got the power to
'spress em as brother Paul did–er, for p'raps he was a better
preecher than I am–er–my feelinks is we all ort tu be jined
to Christ–gist as the husban leeves his father an mother an
is jined tu his wife–er–This is one o'the importantest questions that ever the mind o'man was called to take action
on–er–These things is misteries–er–I allers feels it when
I'm a preechin afore my childring–er they can't compre-
hend it–how we can cry Abby–Father–When we fust try
it's gist like what we read about–er–Dachasier when the
Lord was a passin by–er–he was short o' statier an clim a
sycamore[38]–er–Ef he had a clim sum o'them sycamores in
my settlement–er he'd a hed ruther a tuf time ou 't I'm a
thinkin–now, we mus all try tu clim up tu these things–
Yu see I'm a usin figgers–er–I like figgers when they're
well bro't in–er–Now gentlemen an ladies, as the leetle
chile depends on its mother for nourishment–er so we
mus depend on Jesus Christ–an even tho we may tower
up as high as Manasses, er–or the cedars of Lebanon–
er–or even Mary Magdeleny herself–er–we can't get on
without it–We must cry Abby–Father–man in his inob-
gurateness often has the impunity to appear before his
Maker–without the right sperrit–er–to call on him–Gist
here let me kote one or tu passages o' scripter for yu to medi-
tate on–er–by day or muse on by night–er–"For we are
justified["]–brother Ellis I've done lost it. (whereupon
brother Ellis found & finished it–for him) My breethrin an
sisters things often happens–er–very diff-ren to what we
wud a thot er–ef this ere war ever closes, 'twill be in a
heap differen way to what thousans in these ere United
States thort–er So we will find God des mighty differen–
to what we expect–er–When he brings us to cry out Abby
–Father–But–my breethren an sisters, I can't say no more–

er–I'm clean giv outer (but reviving) one thor't more
come a rushin over me an I feel as though I mus try tu
make it known tu yu–now as none of us knows who of us
now on these ere benches–er–may soon be gone into eter-
nity– before we meet again er you an I may be
thar–er–Thousans as good by natur & better by practise
than we are–er –hev bin suddintly called thar–er–tu
meet thar reward– er–My thort was gentlemen an ladies,
how great a thing God has been allers a doin for man–
er–for when the world was made it took Jesus Christ an
his whole cabinet–er to du it–fur he sed–Let us make
man in our own image–er this shows us that all was fore-
ordained who of us shall–er–cry Abby Father–an who uv
us shall to endless ages uv all past time–er look up frum
the abodes of the damned–er–an hear the orful words
Depart frum me, ye that work iniquity er–May the Lord
help yu tu steer cleer o'that place–may yu live on the
Lord's side–er allers an forever more–er–Breethring an
sisters–I thank you fur your kind intentions to me this
morning–er–I shel try tu cum agin nex time–an now less
sing all jinin in tu the words as I line 'em out–

> Rouse thee my soul, fly up an run,
> Thru every heavenly street–

'Fore we begin, let me say that Brother Ellis will talk to
you–an hev a foot-washin probberble after an hour's
noonin–Sing–Rouse–

There were fine carriages under the trees outside whose
owner's curiosity like our own had brought them to see
this strange ceremony–but we all were doomed to disap-
pointment–as too many outsiders were present–for the
humility even of Hard Shell Baptists–

Nov. 11th. A glorious day this has been–the quiet dropping of
the leaves being the only music. I went alone into the deep
woods & sat listening a long time–There is something indescribably sad to me–when–"The melancholy days are
come" & yet the quiet in these days of turmoil is refreshing

—This one I have watched from the *morning twilight*—"In
that leaden crisis in the four and twenty hours when the
vital force of all the noblest & prettiest things that live is
at its lowest," till the hour when "The sun wraps his robes
around him Closor—like to die"—There has been nothing to
remind one of the world so full of work to do—Nature is
all around going to her short winter's sleep—The ground is
strewn with brilliant orange & crimson leaves, whose beauty
always calls to my mind the hectic flush of consumption—
most beautiful in its decay—The flowers too—are the gayest
of the whole year—gentian asters, & the flaunting red cardinal flower—with the trees everywhere sending out the
long vines which cling to them—now loaded with scarlet
& purple berries—The cotton fields are "white for the harvest"—and one more year is nearly over—Will it close before
this terrible war is settled—Now, there is a lull in the sounds
which grate so on our ears—battle & death On such a day
as this has been it is hard to realize that soldiers are tromping over soil which may ere long be reddened with their
blood, or under which many a poor fellow will sleep his
last sleep—after his last battle has been fought.

Jan 4th, 1863 News reaches us to that *Abraham Lincoln President
of the United States* has on Jan. 1st issued a *proclamation*, declaring "all persons held as slaves within any State, or any
designated part of a State, the people whereof shall then be
in rebellion against the United States, shall be then, there-
after, & thenceforward & forever free"—It is laughed at here
—as the powerless words of an ignorant man[39]—With no
means of knowing how much it may bode to the South,
save my own honest convictions, I cannot but feel that we
may live to see these words literally fulfilled—I shrink from
the future which must come to us ere it is so—from the
possibilities involved in it—To me it seems impossible for
this poor exhausted land long to sustain itself against such
odds—yet were it my native soil "nil desperandum" would
be my watchword—I feel every hour how natural is the
strength of love which one has for a birth-place—God grant
that I may yet see "my own, my nativeland" and find un-

touched by the hand of Death, those who are ever nearest
and dearest to my heart—

Waverley April 24th—We are just getting breath again after a grand
scare—A large body of Yankees have come from nobody
knows where, nobody knows how many, where they were
going, what they came for, or in fact anything at all definite—except the bare fact—they were Yankees—whether
they could speak English or not—they wore blue coats—&
were in a hurry—ordered their meals peremptorily—to be
ready in "double quick time"—borrowed all the fast horses
which fell in their way—as well as poultry of all kinds[40]—
Happening to be in town, on the eventful night, 16th, was
detained nearly a week—it was barricaded with cotton bales
—across the streets—'by order of the Provost Marshal[']—
sentinels posted & no passes given—Silver disappeared rap-
idly—down deep in its mother earth has gone many a family relic—placed there by trembling hands—On going to our
Gen. of militia for a pass—I said, you have given your first
permission to cross the fortifications to a Yankee—Gen.
Harris—He laughed as he said "it is not of such as you we
are afraid"—Found the ferry boat had been sunk—so we
crossed the river in a skiff—found one general commotion
had been the order of the day—It is subsiding—A Yankee
force has passed swiftly through this part of Miss—halted
only 10 miles from here at West Point—"nobody hurt"—is
all we know—Men as well as "helpless women & children["]
were—scared sille—

May 8th Have been three weeks in sole charge of the place—
with 18 servants—no other grown white person—At first,
the responsibility of carrying keys—"giving out" provisions
every day for so many seemed heavy—Soon, night was the
only time when I thought of it—then, "tired nature's sweet
restorer" didn't always come to aforesaid nature and in lieu
thereof come sundry & various imaginations of footsteps
on the piazzas—whispers in the halls—&tc &tc ad infini-
tum. "Uncle Colin" the old carriage driver having professed
to be constantly on the alert "looking out for everybody

on de lot" it was the cause of deep regret when on calling
him he came up missing—Of course next morning he was
surprised exceedingly, was convinced fully—that my only
way was to do as euchre players do—"go it alone"—Except a
narrow escape from burning the smoke house—no accident
has happened—The major domo—alias Lieut. Hamilton of
the Confederate army—(who raised a company of poor
men, went to the battle of Shiloh, found it did not suit his
constitution to be where gunpowder was so freely used, resigned at once, took an indefinite furlough,—which has
never expired, & is not likely to) is back with Madam who
takes the keys today[41]—The old cook Amelia said this
morning—"mistress, dese is de mos plesentest three weeks
we ever been had on dis lot—God knows." A permanent
responsibility of this kind I would not have for worlds—
this has been enough to satisfy me—

June 1st Summer is here again with intense oppressive heat the
grass is scorched & dry—corn fields look as though a fire
had passed quickly over them. The early morning is our
only time for any comfort, days drag wearily along—in the
attempt to do duty—The only war news is continuation of
the siege of Vicksburg—which our papers say can never be
taken—though it is acknowledged that Gen. Grant is a
"mighty man of valor"[42]—There is no comfort in this disturbed aimless existence—Reading is impossible. It is far
from pleasant to hear continual expressions of vituperation
against all Yankees—& be obliged to let them pass as if unheard—but so it must be, Daily & how my prayer goes
forth—that this may soon be over—

July 8th Again we hear of total defeat—On the morning of the
4th—Vicksburg surrendered—To me this seems an unmistakeable proof of "manifest destiny"—what sooner or later
must be the end of this terrible "inexpressible conflict" The
tide which ebbed so strongly towards the South in the beginning, and filled all hearts with proud exultation—now
flows all another way—But as the Mohammedans when
sorrow overtakes them so must we say —Allah wills it—His
name be praised—

Diary of Caroline Seabury

[Caroline inserted into her diary the following letter of introduction.]

Tunica Co Miss, Aug 10th 1863

Judge Venable
My Dear Sir—
    Allow me to introduce to you Miss Seabray of Columbus Miss, formerly of New York—Miss S is desirous of getting back to her relatives in N.Y. and she may need some assistance while in your City, in the way of advice. Knowing you to be fully capable of advising her I have taken the liberty and pleasure of introducing you—Hoping your acquaintance may be mutually agreeable I remain most truly
Your friend
E. W. Dale

24th—Today saw a *country barbecue* & *wedding*, a feast given when the crop is "laid by" so far as working it goes—"fodder pulling" is over—and a day of rejoicing is given the negroes—when they have a merry making on their own account. with abundance of fruits, barbecued pig, mutton &tc—to which they do ample justice—"The white folks" were first entertained at the long table—a crowd of eager faces surrounding us as we were helped—That was soon over, & we retired to a respectful distance to look on—There was every variety of second hand finery, flowers, ribbons, & laces, party dresses which "young mistis" had doffed in days gone by—sometimes it bore marks of rejuvenating but oftener—they were all untouched by any hand but "old Time"—a pyramid of flowers over kinky hair—or an enormous wreath of all colors & sizes of flowers, intermingled with everything shiny imaginable or rather available—The "genmen" were arrayed in a gorgeousness fully to correspond with their fair sisters—vests and neck ties were of every gay color & pattern—large pins and watch chains, as well as rings on their fingers—glittered in profusion—Their politeness to each other on "dress parade" occasions is overwhelming—It is a native instinct with them and it knows no bounds. A French dancing master might take lessons in graceful bows—After the eating was duly performed, one division walked off to a level spot where the sound of bones & banjo soon

set their feet in motion and for a half hour muscles of the
entire "physicality" knew had no rest from their labor—
twisting, turning, jumping everywhere. Affectionate as the
waltz always is, they put to the blush all white attempts to
equal their ardor—From one of the cabins we herd a hymn
being sung, and found that the "Christians was a havin'
meetin" Master & Mistis with their friends were invited in
& an impressive sight it was—an old white headed negro
soon rose & after a short exhortation—prayed, in fervent
though disconnected words—which often called forth loud
amens God grant it—from the rest—and I could not but
think that it might reach His ear—who has said "Come unto me all ye who labor, & are heavy laden"—Music is worship to them, and they seemed to me filled with the spirit
of both—as their voices grew louder & fuller in the revival
songs—After an hour's "meeting" they adjourned for a
"weddin"—in another cabin—The bride was coal black but
adorned most elaborately even to tumbled orange flowers
and a veil—the groom a bright mulatto being a carriage
driver was in a full suit of black—The minister with an
air of pomposity which would defy description—in a loud
tone ordered them to "jine der hands"—then in a voice
of volume both "deep and loud" he prayed for everything
concievable—at last, "that de lord Jesus would take care
of dis couple, till dey is separated apart, an took up into
glory"—Then the usual question,—"does any of you know
anything agin this man an woman being jined"—Ef you
don't speak now—keep it back allers & forever—Nobody
spoke. then began—"Will you Chales be married onto
Maria, an lub her, an take care of her an be good to her,
as long as you ken live together"⁴³ Charles willed, and to
Maria—"Will you promise fore God an dis sassembly to lub
him, an honor him, and rebay him, as long as you can"—
Maria assented blushingly we supposed though invisibly
then louder yet he announced "You is now husban an wife
—Pollute your bride"—which was followed by a general
rush for congratulations—and which we retired outside the
door—Soon the Rev. roared out—"Is dere anybody else dat
wants to get married"—["]if not, dis congregation is dis-

missed"–He wiped his polished ebony face–& waited for a
response–but, not long, for out stepped two hand in hand
dressed in plantation suits–the groom looked as though
"unexpectedly called on" to officiate in that capacity. Being
only "common hands" few words were used,–they only
"jinin hands" and promising to live together in peace so
long as they could–which "mistis" told me they had done
for years–but, they had got religion and wanted to be
married now–No more presenting themselves–we left for
the cabin where supper was ready–the logs were decked
with cedar branches sprinkled with flowers to look bridal–
the first reminder of a snow-storm I had seen in a long
time–Old "Uncle Prime" was doing duty as watchman
over the supper which was a contribution from each of the
guests–I asked Uncle P. how old he was–he said "I don'
know mistis"–but I'm nigh onto 200 I 'spex"–Eating with
us was a mere ceremony–but not so with the Rev. brother
who advanced as we left–and went vigorously to work
right and left[.] We left the brides following his example–
they were all for one day at least–in the negroe's heaven–
with plenty to eat and good clothes to wear–no work to
be done–

Waverly–Miss. July 20th

Almost for the first time in my life–this summer time
hangs heavily on my hands for lack of something to busy
both mind and body. With nothing to sew, because there
is no material to be had, except as now & then a call is
made for soldier's clothes. Even after learning to twist on a
"great wheel," there is nothing left to twist–A new book I
have not seen in two years, nor even heard what has been
published in Yankee land–nothing has been here. Believing fully in the old maxim, "Satan finds some mischief still
for idle hands to do," & fearing I might illustrate its truth,
I have been reduced to the last semblance of occupation–
patch-work–in company with my friends here–a last resort
in the hour of extremity–The intense heat and an uneasy
mind make study impossible, or that would be an exhaustless resource–This year and a half of waiting to hear some-

thing from the land of my birth–& those I love–has
dragged along and when will the perfect work of patience
be accomplished–May the work of these hours never in
the future cover a sleeper whose dreams shall be haunted
by the spirits of unrest and weariness which surround me
today–

Night July 28th 1863 Waverley, Lowndes Co. Miss
After long dreary months of watching and waiting, trying
in vain to get a "pass through the lines" of military rule,
listening to the stories of others who have failed in the
attempt–an unexpected opportunity has presented itself.
Though it seems almost "hope against hope" tomorrow
morning I start–leaving a desolate country, breaking associations which have been the result of year's companionship–some of joy–others of the bitterest grief–bidding
perhaps a last farewell to the dear spot where I have so
often found fresh flowers strewn by unknown hands–I
have left it to their kind remembrance–will it be forgotten
amid the confusion of constantly recurring death scenes in
this terrible war–That has been my only quiet retreat–God
only knows the prayers which have gone up from my heart
there–He alone tonight sees the secrets which have me
thus long to stay here–with no sympathy in the cause of
the war–secession–believing the principle–or rather its
total lack of it wrong–personal rather than any political
reasons–have been the "moving why." Nearly three years
have passed away since I saw the land of my birth, and my
friends there–none but those whose treasures of friendship
are divided, can realize how a woman's heart and judgment
are divided with them–I know nothing of the true state of
things North–with no father's house, to which I could
turn without a thought of doubt, no mother whose arms
would be open to recieve me, no sister to give me the kiss
of welcome, with only one dear brother far up in the North-
west–I have for years felt homeless everywhere–sometimes
almost from my soul, uttering poor Hood's "anywhere,
anywhere out of the world"–which has seemed so cold
and lonely–Now, Providence seems plainly saying "This is

the way, walk ye in it"–Whither it will lead He only knows who holds all issues in His Omnipotent hand–There are no sounds out in the silver moonlight save the whippoor-will's plaintive cry–As I think of the possibilities which to-morrow may bring with it–I well nigh falter–but–in this still hour–there comes a consciousness of spiritual presence –those gone to the other land–seem to be around me–I can almost hear their gentle whisper, see their radiant faces coming as they have in so many dark hours, with messages of comfort–and support–bringing what I so much need– that which will strengthen my weak faith–assurance of His love whose servants they are–teaching me ever to recieve

> "All as God wills, who wisely heeds
> To give or to withold
> And knoweth more of all my needs
> Than all my prayers have told"

Monday morning July 29th 1863

The message yesterday evening was "have the lady & her baggage at the meeting house by the cross-roads at 5 to-morrow morning" Long before that the household of my friends Gen. & Mrs. Gerdine[?] was all astir–A hasty break-fast was gone through with, the kissing over with "the white folks," good-bye's to the numerous darker ones who were crowded around us, as they always do when an event is expected–The family carriage took "mistress" the two lit-tle one & myself, "master" on horseback, with the baggage going ahead–A few minutes driving brought us to the trysting place in the "piney woods." The thermometer stood at 85° when we left home. This did not promise to be a cool undertaking in any sense of the word–Punctual-ity in this latitude forms no part of the list of positive vir-tues–We women had time to say our "last words"–albeit some tell us such things are only myths–the reality never being manifest–Many a message to father, and sisters at home, from the Northern wife whose love was divided from the Southern husband–"tell the Yankees they haven't whipped us yet, if they have got Vicksburg and Fort Hud-son–and Gettys-burg too." Since his son had come from

Vicksburg a paroled prisoner two days before, barefoot, hungry—and having walked 150 miles, from want of both money and any mode of conveyance, and given glowing accounts of Yankee resources, I thought his courage had recovered a little, as to the end—but, in words at least he was unfaltering—From this beginning of final messages some hostile words might have soon grown, had not we heard the tromping of horses feet up the road, then the lumbering of a wagon—soon there emerged from the underbrush, a stout red-faced jolly specimen of humanity—on a refractory mule—His "good mornin to yes" had brogue from "Sweet Erin"—which we seldom heard—next behind him rode up a meek jaded, guant [gaunt] individual, who nodded silently, and halted, then 4 independent care for nobody-looking mules trotted up—Then my carriage—drawn by 4 mules. Seated on the back of one was my driver a "yellow boy" Jack—In the rear came Mr. Stone, my protector, who had come up with his cattle, and now was returning for his family—trying to place them all beyond the reach of Yankees —My trunks were soon deposited in the back of the capacious wagon, my "split bottom" chair next went in, "positively the last" words were said, and then came an operation which at first threatened to prove a "nolle prosequi" to farther operations—getting in the passenger. This must be accomplished by mounting the forward wheel, thence by one long step farther—the top was reached. After sundry failures showing too plainly that I was unused to lofty flights, Dan's brawny Irish arm came to my assistance, he comforting me by saying, "N'ver mind ye'll soon get used to it, shure, an not care a bit for it, like the Irishmen bein hung"—I was landed safely and at half past 6 we started—A survey of my domain showed me as a back-ground my trunks—next the chair & occupant, by my side the box of provisions for the week, thanks to my friends at Waverley I had everything necessary—Next in front of me, were "sundries"—blankets, cooking utensils, ropes, axes, and a gun—strongly suggestive in these war times—An extra saddle did me good service as a footstool—Over half the wagon was stretched a cloth cover—A half hour's ride explained fully

Diary of Caroline Seabury

the meaning of Mr. Stone's first questions after I had asked
him to take me back with him–"did you ever ride in a
wagon without springs, could you stand it for six days over
poor roads do you think?" I thought my experiences of the
ups and downs in Dixie life in the last two years, had prepared my mind for anything but–being now and then
summarily deposited among the "sundries" had not entered into my plans–Picking oneself up under the most
favorable circumstances is not a pleasant recreation, when
there is every prospect of frequent repetition it becomes
less so–After the first few miles–we got into "perares"
mind–and here I was not so often called upon to "change
my base of operations" as the war phrase goes–There was
nothing to be done but drag along through the black road
–nothing to be seen to change the current of one's
thoughts–A cloudless sky made the world look brighter–
in the beginning of what to most would have seemed "a
leap in the dark"–it was really "flying from ills we have, to
those we know not of."–The refusal of Gen. Ruggles to
give me a pass had given him "a place in my memory," and
I fervently wished that he might be jolted enough in his
future career, to make him repent his obduracy and see
that nothing was gained by him a Yankee born in Massachusetts, by such extra efforts to prove his extreme loyalty
to the Southern cause. So many obstacles apparently insur-
mountable had been overcome, that I had become convinced of the truth of Napoleon's life maxim "To a firm
faith and determined will there are no impossibilities["]
Providence had pointed out to me this means of reaching
Federal lines–A convex mirror seemed before my mind's
eye–enlarging all the blessings in my present surroundings
–Gradually my novel equipage and outriders began to call
forth incipient emotions of pride–when we reached West
Point 10 miles journey at noon I was for the first time conscious of being the ["]observed of all observers," not very
pleasantly so to be sure–Here it was necessary to get a pass
to Panola. Mr Stone asking for mine as a friend going to
visit his wife, a slight fiction, as a week before I had never
heard of him or his wife–[(]though my friends had). On

83

giving my name a gentleman standing by said, "It is a pity Miss S is going way down there on such a hard journey for she'll not get through to the North she may be sure," Mr. S. coolly replying "I only ask a pass to Panola" stopped further remarks. Of this unknown sympathizer I at the time knew nothing but, I had become used to the saying "We don't blame you for wanting to go, but you'll never get through the lines" &tc—It only strengthened my woman's resolution. Under cover of my long gray calico sunbonnet I had been "plaiting" palmetto—an accomplishment taught me the day I decided to come this way—this was the fancy work of Southern ladies—now, and I flattered myself it was the finishing touch to my thorough disguise as a country woman—Mr. S. having cautioned me to let him do the talking everywhere—West Point was swarming with soldiers —in all sorts of uniforms & all stages of happiness, all "calvary's" as the negroes say—some dismounting without orders or intention to do so, some charging the zig-zag fences, one officer evidently "conquered not by superior numbers," but very inferior whisky—was being supported by two privates who were trying to get him on his horse— they were all hurrahing & whooping—calling on the ——— Yankees to come up—They were under orders to reinforce Gen. Chalmers—who had started in pursuit of a "large body of Yankees" who were "coming down"[44]—Slow travelers these same Yankees must be—for a year they have been coming and we have never seen them yet—It was a relief to plod through the mud—& get outside the town limits, for it seemed to me like a glimpse of Pandemonium—We dragged along through a poor country, inhabited by the same class of people—with no men under the conscript age—45 yrs. at home—except here and there one wounded or otherwise disabled—It was not the region for the "last ditch" men—I had seen their homes, and been in the family of a lieutenant for a year who had an unlimited furlough, and had been a "volunteer aid" to Gen. Price—with his body-servant he had "defended his hearth-stone" sitting by it, when not hunting or fishing—after raising a company of poor men to fight for their nativeland three rich brothers in law—acting the same parts – I had seen the rich side of this war only – except in the hospitals – The other side of the picture began to show itself – even in this one day's journey – Late in the evening we stopped for corn, at the first comfortable looking house I had seen outside of the few at West Point. I was urged to get out during the operation of loading but, recalling my experience in the morning's climb, preferred remaining – so round to the corn crib we drove – & the business of depositing a day's supply of food for our mules was going on in front of my seat – when to my surprise the head of an old acquaintance appeared – He was owner of the place, & with his wife, came to insist upon my coming to the house – but I told them that would be going back – which I did not like to do ever – so they spent the half hour with me – Though a young man, he had the good fortune to half an inch difference in the length of his legs, & was exempt. As he understood my destination – there was no danger in declaring himself "strong Union from the start, never for secession &tc – now for reconstruction" – the grounds of which we had not settled when "all ready master" was the signal for us to be off – a few delicious watermelons being added to our commissary department – Before night we met a long train of people "running from the Yankees" – They were preceded by the wagons, containing the bedding, clothing, & provisions – interspersed promiscuously therein were the children too small to walk – their woolly heads peeping out from under the cover – some of them with pale faces and blue eyes – the most pitiable of all sights in a land of slavery – The oldest men and women being left to take care of themselves at home as we were told "it would not pay to take them away" Behind the wagons came a motley assemblage of all shades of color, their faces expressing little but stolid indifference to their fate – "Master & Mistes['] with their family and the overseer – followed at some distance to prevent "straggling" – A few dogs were with them in case of emergency – It recalled a terrible fright I once had when walking alone in the woods, & hearing a pack of their coming in full chase – their yelling was unlike any other bark I ever heard – I was told on reaching home,

that my fears were groundless, as they never attacked white
people–These were some "common white folks" not the
poor class–yet not the F.F's[45]–The panic had siezed them
–"Yankees is comin"–and they were going–"Isn't you
feerd to go where dey is Mistis,["] one of the old women
asked me–all our white folks is–Of course they professed
to be so too–One of the men asked me if "dey reely is got
horns on em?["] When I told him I was one–his eyes rolled
about in blank amazement. After a minute he replied
coolly–"I doesn't bleeve dat mistis, you's jes like our white
folks."–He had so long heard the horned head of all evil,
and the Yankees called by the same epithet, that he believed them identical in species. "You can tell a Yankee as
far you can see them" were familiar words–everywhere–he
perhaps thought horns were the distinctive mark. failing to
discover these–he believed me "playing possum"–their
most emphatic way of expressing deciet–for no other animal is so skilled in its use–When I asked them where they
were going, some said, "De Lord knows, we don't,["] &
"we's gis runnin away from de Yankees somewhar."–Master
done started for Souf Caliny,–or Georgy–They were going
from home to avoid the "Manifest Destiny" of the system
of slavery–believing that the proclamation of Mr. Lincoln
was only a dead letter, hoping yet to sit under their own
vine and fig tree as of yore–& "making cotton" again in
Miss.[46] Not a very long time hence, the question must be
decided if the occasional hints we get of "want of provisions" &tc in our army mean anything–As twilight came
on, we stopped to get a resting-place for the night–once
we were answered by a grim hard faced woman, "we hain't
no man here, he's gone to the war, and scacely anything
ourselves to eat, let alone feedin rank strangers"–another
miserable old man, sitting by his cabin door said, "thar
ain't nobody but me an the women folks to make a crop,
conscrips took 'em all away–an God knows were bad off
enough–A barefooted boy about 16 hobbled out on a
rude crutch–one leg was gone apparently not long ago–
for he was unused to the loss of it. We went on seeing the
same thriftless class of "poor white folks" who in ordinary

times barely make a living by labor on the sandy soil–in
war time even that was hardly possible–At length after the
moon had for two hours been giving us the light of her
countenance we came to a double log-cabin in the "piney
woods" where they "took in strangers"–and, we soon
found it literally true I emerged from my retreat, found as
is generally the case, it is much easier to get down than up
into high positions in life. We crossed the rail fence of our
host's front yard, recieved the usual salute of yelping curs,
and were met by the lord of the manor, with a "howd'ye"
["]set down"–The space between the two rooms was filled
nearly by soldiers waiting for supper–purporting to be paroled men from Fort Hudson, probably deserters from
Johnson's Army–They soon left much to my relief–I was
escorted into "the room"–a dim torch light was flickering
in the fire-place. There was one servant about, who came
in with "light wood" now & then, she told me "mistis
couldn't come in now, she's gittin you all's supper in de
kitchen"–In due season, that was accomplished, and the
lady appeared–bringing with here a much needed light–
only more pines, for even tallow candles were a tabooed
luxury. She loomed up in the glare of light–a genuine
Meg Merrills[47]–only lacking the determination of her
face–She reminded of hearing a poor woman once say she
"had allers had to rub up against the world" and this one
looked as though all had got rubbed out but her bones.
and few clothes were left to cover them–Her invitation
to "take a bite" I could not muster courage to accept. Telling her I had provisions, with me, but was very tired &
wanted sleep–made no visible impression on her–With
arms akimbo, she stood asking me all manner of questions
as deliberately as though I were in a prisoner's box. Ain't
you jes meeried to this y'er man–you must be to be gwine
down there–ain't ye feerd o' the Yankees, till I was out of
patience & told her I was too tired to talk. "Well, I spose
likely you be, I reckon I better fix yer bed"–Leaving me
alone for a minute, I took a survey of things in general–
which showed me three beds one unoccupied, the second
contained a woman and child sick with "the ager"–the

third contained a half-grown boy—On the reappearance
of madam the door was shut, which was done by drawing
a calico curtain across the door-way—this had in it not a
few holes of divers sizes—not strange when we think calico
now is selling from $2,50 to $4,19 pr. yard—and money
just as hard for the poor to get as it ever was. Next, the
strong sinewy arm was brought to bear upon the lubberly
boy—& the shrill voice sounded out "Jim I say, you git up,
an give the lady your bed,"—but he was snoring too loudly
to respond—& not until after a vigorous application of her
bony hand, in a manner with which maternal authority everywhere is wont to enforce itself—in the early years of life,
did said Jim realize the situation—An unconditional surrender was the result—he retreated in quick time if not good
order into the other room.—Soon, I was informed that
the bed was ready—The light was gone—or "tired Nature's
sweet restorer," would never have been sought there, for
scarcely had my aching head touched the scantily filled
pillows when an ominous odor greeted me—with which all
travelers are so wofully familiar—A reconnaissance by moonlight was soon made—numberless little mahogany colored
spots were changing places in all directions—"Overcome by
the force of vastly superior numbers" as our army has so
often been in reports, "with which we felt it would be useless to contend the field was abandoned"—A chair leaned
against the logs was my substitute, in a few minutes I was
wandering to a land where the poets tell us soft music fills
the air, and every breeze is freighted with sweet odors.
How long this dreaming lasted, I could not tell, but, O,
what a wakening was there—strange sounds came up from
the corner bed I last saw vacant—at first I thought some
one was in terrible agony—and sprang up to relieve it—but
—there lay placid as the moonbeams playing over their
faces—the host & hostess with open mouths seeming to be
vying with each other in "making night hideous"—both by
sight and sound—Here ended my sleep—for that was unbroken music till morning. Its first dawning was joyfully
welcomed, & improved in getting ready for an exit—The
reason given by madam for the status of things was—"we

hain't got no water under quarter o'a mile from here,"–
Gladly did I emerge from that first night's experience of
the indoor life of "poor white folks" in Chickasaw, realiz-
ing that they did in very fact–"take in strangers"–

30th   Dan, the Irishman, had our breakfast ready before sunrise–
with a log serving for both seat and table, a cup of coffee,
some bread and ham were soon disposed of–The mules
were quietly eating near us–Our entire cuisine arrange-
ments consisted of a frying pan, & an old tin coffee pot–
even genuine Yankee ingenuity could hardly have made the
pan serve more purposes in half an hour–The invaluable
box was replaced by my side in the wagon, other things all
went in front, by 5 the mounting this time had been accomplished much more easily–and we were off–hoping to
make 35 miles before bed-time. Jack was unable to rouse
any latent ambition in our mules–by his persuasive "git,
git" and flourishing the long whip he held over them–
Their susceptibility to this argument seems blunted by its
frequent use–out of a walk they would not go. Not a little
fun was made for us all by Dan–who losing patience with
his animal would belabor him in Irish style, notwithstand-
ing Jack's cautious, "mas'a Dan mules is mules–dey won't
go no faster den dey want to, an you can't make em no
how"–Twice his efforts resulted in a downfall–and some
very emphatic remarks on the nature of mules in general–
Poor Dan, the certainty of failure seems never to have
taught his race caution–He kept trying–and failing–to
conquer the unconquerable–but, before night–Jack's remark that "niggers knows best how to manage 'em,–jes let
em alone"–seemed to carry conviction with it–either that
or the falls he had got–for he rode resignedly on as any of
us–In a southern summer's day there is a feeling of mis-
using them even though it is only dragging along–Unflat-
tering though the comparison be, I thought there was a
striking similarity between our progress and that of the
Yankees in their late victories–slow but sure–I could not
read without pain to my eyes–so kept my palmetto turning into braid–A flock of wild turkeys appeared once, and

were out of sight in quick time—More trains of people running or being run from Yankees met us—all telling the same story—"they leave nothing alive on the place, steal jewelry—and money"—and worst of all "run off the niggers"—their crops except wheat were yet in the field—they going to States which had had already passed laws forbidding any more slaves to be brought there—"as there is already great scarcity of food." They were reaping the harvest which the originators of secession sowed broad-cast—one which those opposed to it foresaw but could hardly realize its extent—and who can tell where it will end—One hope after another has failed the Confederacy—"foreign intervention," the ignis fatuus which somebody has kept dancing before the eyes of politicians has lost its power in recruiting the wasted armies—Vicksburg was declared impregnable but is gone—It has thrown a pall over everything in the tone of even their boasting now—there is an echo of despair—In these long journeys without even the ordinary comforts of life—many must die—This whole country is groaning under the burdens slavery has brought on it—which can never be taken away until the words of the song which now seem such a mockery here—shall be literally true—["]The star-spangled shall wave o'er the land of the free"—black as well as white—

At our dinner today on a log in the woods, I found my love for the old Union no stronger than had my friend Mr Stone—but, he frankly said I could not say as much to a Southerner safely—or to any one at home—I can not find words to express my hatred of secession from the beginning.—

This was a "long, long weary day"—but I did not "pass it in tears away" for I kept plaiting and thinking—to-night we'll pitch our wagon A days march nearer—["]Yankee land"—home I could not say—as does the hymn—The poor woman where we stopped for water at noon—expressed what in these two days had become a conviction with me. "This is the rich folk'es war,"—She went on—["]I've got only one child, & I want him to come home and take care o'me—and stop fightin for them—he's got wounded once now—an we've got no niggers to work for us"—This was the other side of a story I had heard one way only—and it was pitiful enough—There was the cold reality of this "war for independence"—at every poor man's home we saw—and there were no others on our route thus far. Just at dark we rode up to a two-story "frame house["] painted white— belonging Mr. Stone told me to "Squire Clayton["]—of Calhoun Co. The look of comfort about everything was refreshing—Dan rode up and echoed my thoughts—"Shure, ye'll not be fightin here as ye did the last night—I'm thinkin Miss, ye'll be the better of a night's rest"—Mr. S— quietly remarked as we went up the walk—"they're sharp here—let me do the talking—we'll tell the same story—they know me well"—I was introduced as "a friend on a visit"— to four young ladies—Squire C. and wife, and a wounded son a Colonel—just from Vicksburg—As the war question is the only subject of conversation—soon all were engaged— fortunately supper was announced—I was too tired to eat, and very soon excused myself—and retired—not to rest at once, for in came the young ladies one by one, questioning me with a persistency which would have done honor to the far famed inquisitiveness of a Vermonter—Their aston- ishment at my daring to go to "the bottom" where Yankees were, was boundless, and their expressions of bitterness were choice English to say the least—They asked if I had any brothers in the army, telling me about one killed, and the wounded one, who wasn't going in again for "pa's got him a substitute for the war"—Then they showed me cloths they had spun and woven for themselves—saying "I'll wear homespun as long as I live before I'd depend on Yankees for it—wouldn't you"? Of course, I said I would—Finding that there was plenty of water here, I asked to have a bath, and excused my sleepiness by telling them my last night's encounter,—so in process of time, I was left alone—to enjoy two of the greatest luxuries to a traveler—cold water—and sleep—"Now I lay me," was soon said—and the "action suited to the word"—

31st My next conscious minute was when Mr. S. rapped on my door in the morning saying "we're waiting breakfast for you, and want to get an early start"—My gray calico dress

& bonnet were soon donned, and before our host & host-
esses of the night were up we had breakfasted in camp, &
were off–The sun rose with promise of the hottest day we
had felt, and we were not disappointed–The way was over
a more hilly country–harder traveling–but nothing of interest–in the scenery–Mr. S. and the two others went
ahead Jack and I were alone for half the day–He giving me
a graphic account of "bein took by de Yankees twice down
by de riber, an runnin back to Master"–but I'll tell you jes
what I thinks mistis–said he–["]dey'll whip us all clean
out fore we done–though white folks says dey dont think
so–I seen 'em, I been dar, I know dey can–an dey's never
g'wine to giv it up till they do"–About 4 P.M. we came to
Coffee-ville where last winter a large depot on the Miss.
Central Road, and some other buildings were burned by a
retreating force of Yankees. The field where a skirmish took
place was pointed out to us. soon we saw large black patches
on the ground, with fleeces of cotton lying around–it was
burned "to prevent its falling into the hands of our enemy"
–Here was the first I had seen of the savages of war, except
on humanity. It seemed like going back to the past which
we read of–in other lands, but no part of our own–"Military necessity" is the plea for much which seems utterly
useless waste of men and property–The tall black chimneys
stood like so many spectres–hovering about the still village
which had no appearance of life in the streets–I was thankful when "Night let down her curtain" for the heat had
been intensely oppressive, and the last few hour's scenery
no less so to the mind–It was eleven before we got a resting-place–Everybody was suspicious of strangers–and
made some excuse us shelter. At last, through Dan's di-
plomacy alias–Irish fibbing there was "rest for the weary"
found under the roof of an old lady–she having been told
that "a sick lady was behind, and could go no farther–
niver a mile without rest." Ignorant of his fabrication, I
wondered at the woman's hurry in preparing my room,
asking me if I felt better &tc–she, poor soul, trying to
imagine it possible for me to be sick–At last–she said–"la
me, that man was just foolin me, to get in"–and I laughed

as heartily as she when she told me the story—The men
and beasts were camped near the house always—We sat
down in the bright moon light and with a trembling voice
and tears streaming down her cheeks this mother told me
how two sons had been killed—the last one was a cripple
living with her, and "the old man"—with his wife and two
children—"he's worse than crippled too she said, for he's
learned to drink in the army"—Poor before the war—now
helpless and hopeless they were—In other countries there
are avenues open to the same class of people—here—what
can they do—This side of the question has been carefully
kept concealed by all who have magniloquently written
and spoken of what "The Sunny South will be when we
gain our Independence"—If that day ever came, of what
avail can it be to the poor? They have unresistingly submit-
ted to being ridden over by the power of money—so long
as there is slavery, they will be only a grade higher in the
social scale than those who are bought and sold legitimately.
Southern rulers never have come from this class and never
will—until "great change comes oe'r the spirit of their
dreams"—My own that night were unbroken after a ride of
16 hours—only resting an hour for dinner—Next morning
we were [*sentence unfinished*]

August 1st I woke with a new feeling of vigor, for in time, we
were half through our "tedious and tasteless" journey—
more than half in distance—even with the gait of mules we
had gone 100 miles.—Before sunrise we had bid the old
folks good bye—breakfasted in the woods, and started on—
found a shady road, quite in contrast with the red clay—
most of yesterday without trees.—At noon we came to the
Yokney [Yocona] river at Greenwood where last winter a
fine bridge was burned. We crossed on a flatboat—and dined
in a beautiful grove of cottonwood and gum trees. in sight
of the ruins—somewhat in contrast with the Greenwood of
so many sacred memories—but a pretty spot for even an
artist's eye—While we were sitting here, a gentleman rode
up—whom Mr. Stone knew—he told us that the Yankees
were coming now "sure enough"—A body of them nobody

knew how many, had landed three days before, from a gunboat. on the Miss. and were "just taking every-thing before them"–Mr. S. thought it a "fresh scare," but concluded to go ahead as scout–as in case we met them, our mules and provisions would all be taken–if nothing more was done–He left me–only telling me I could do more for him, than he for me–perhaps, if the worst came–Dan– was quite unconcerned. He told me he had in one pocket "a small bit o' paper which would serve him a good turn" if he met them which I understood was the oath of allegiance[48]–He had been into the country from Memphis selling cotton cards at $30 a pair–and was there a strong secessionist–talking loudly of the fights he was in &tc–but never telling on which side–Having about my person the little all of my own money, and about $700 going to Canada for a friend, I had a strange feeling of dread when I thought of meeting Yankees–as all Union soldiers go by that name, whether they can speak a word of English or not. To a woman alone in a strange country, in wartime, with a negro, an Irishman, and a poor scared individual whose only thought was to keep in the rear and so be protected–the prospect was rather dubious–but, there was no alternative being unable to whistle to keep my courage up as boys do, I had only to–sit still–That after all, is the hardest thing to do in an exciting emergency, and often would be the very best. Towards evening, we met several excited parties but could learn nothing definite–Sometimes there was a big army landed from a boat, then again a squad of "Calvaries"–"making a raid an leavin nothing alive"–["]except the white folks"–so on we went, half doubting–half believing there must be some foundation– some fire to create all this smoke–We stopped six miles from Panola, at a log cabin which recalled forcibly my first night's exploit–in Chickasaw Co. but Mr. S. thought it more prudent to avoid stopping in towns–A bare-footed yellow-haired man appeared on the porch in answer to our "hallos" and asked us to "light"–so we lit on the ground, and told him we must stay there some way–He said "Yre lady-'ll find us mighty poor sir"–["]my ole women'll be out soon though an will try to take care on ye"–Our provision box had held out, so in that line we were independent –"Miss Carson" was soon presented conveying along with her a pair of small twins–resembling strongly their pater– Gradually several more children appeared, of different sizes –but all of the light-long-haired weak eyed type–with as little clothing as could be passed for decent–from oldest to youngest of the family–the father was "six months home on sick furlough" I proposed walking a while before trying to sleep, for a fancy came over me–that "coming events cast their shadows before"–as I glanced round my room– and thought exercise in walking might help to quiet my senses–but the hope was vain–So far as humanity went, I was alone, but–O, the travelers over those logs, over the bed, curtains–myself–were innumerable–Moon light reveries are pretty to talk about, and very enjoyable–sometimes–but under existing circumstances, quite another thing–The only relief–was in the pure bright night–for in a southern rain–what would it have been. I thought of the Spaniard who said he always put on glasses when he ate cherries, to make them look larger, and tried hard to see the best side. Being up all night–I was ready for the day's work before any of our party–

2nd I had laid my watch on the table, and "mine hostess" appeared with the dawn, that was something of which she could not understand the use–having never seen a timepiece–"we allers goes by de sun–she told me–an when it rains–we knows any how nigh enuf for poor folks."–She had breakfast ready in time–and in her own room–two of the children were asleep–things generally thoroughly disgusting She begged for my faded calico dress, till I started to walk in advance of the wagon–Her "du eat if yer kin eat our vittels"–had induced me to make sundry fruitless attempts so to do–and I tried the Beecher philosophy of fresh air and exercise–to carry off my uncomfortable feelings–He says many a blue total depravity sermon has been given to the world because the writer needed to plough it out–into the ground. When our wagon came up, I had gone a mile to the top of a steep hill, a strange sight in this sandy country. The vision of that poor forlorn woman, and the hungry twins—her numberless questions, and the wretched apology for breakfast for which we had paid so roundly had faded away in the fresh morning air—when Dan recalled it in genuine Irish, "An shure miss, since the Lord made me, did iver I set foot in a place the likes o'that intirely—and may He and the blissid Vargin forgive me if iver I do agin, and indade I'll niver have to ask it"—We had but a short ride to Panola, Gen. Chalmer's head-quarters— Here our pass must be renewed. Fresh reports of "Yankees coming" were rife everywhere—the streets of the town were full of soldiers under orders to march none seemed to know where—Mr. Stone sent the wagon on directly through with my outriders he going to the Provost Marshal's office to get a new pass—which was soon accomplished—and we hurried down to the Tallahatchie just in time to cross on the flat-boat before the movement of troops began—Had we been an hour later we would have probably waited at least three days for them—In the thick cotton-woods through which our route lay—we met several small companies of men going to join Gen. C. At any other time the sudden appearance of a dozen horsemen riding at full speed through a dense forest would have been startling—but, their non-descript uniforms told us at once they were not the much dreaded "Yankees" and so, we had less to fear—Our poor rear-guard—Mr Sykes could not conceal his fear—he rode slowly along with a general air of shakiness, his long lank figure adding to the effect of the dolorous expression his face wore—Once when he was far behind, we were passing a country grave-yard in a clearing—Dan suggested to Mr S. "wouldn't ye the bether off to stop and take up a dead man & let him change places with yer Misther who's trimbling so bad"—When we were fairly "out of the woods["] his drooping courage seemed to revive—by noon we reached a large clearing where was a cornfield the best we had seen— poor cotton had all along been scattered by the road— though that crop was interdicted by the Confederate gov-ernment—"except to supply actual necessities at home" It had been said that large planters had found it necessary to raise great quantities—in locations out of sight—providing for future emergencies—We got here some cream sent to "the lady" by the mistress of the house near—Few nerves in Dixie land have trembled from the effect of pure coffee, but we enjoyed our Mocha unadulterated with rye—sweet potatoes, or burnt molasses the fashionable substitutes— now in vogue—Ours had been smuggled through from Memphis—in return for cotton—We dined hastily—not quite at ease about the "undiscovered future"—We found better land and more cotton as we rode on—Corn was nearly ready for harvesting—It seemed incredible that in a land where "devotion to the good of our country" is the watchword, in every rich man's mouth, that the land should be made to bring forth what most materially strengthened the "sinews of war" of the enemy—but, here were the proofs —growing—When night came on, we were in dense woods again—almost pathless—Dan & Mr. S went ahead prospect- ing—leaving the silent man, Jack and myself to plod slowly on—The bright moonlight came down through the tall trees, and the birds were all singing their good night song to their mates—all manner of flying things were in the air it seemed to me, as we brushed against the low boughs of undergrowth—At about eleven we came to a clearing—the first we had seen for miles, but—"our corn is all done eat up"—was the reply to our asking for shelter at the house— here was no entertainment for man or beast—a few miles farther on we stopped at some negro cabins—there was no white person on the place. Master was a bachelor an gone to the wars—It was almost midnight when after a survey of the houses, I concluded to stay in the wagon—with my chair leaned against the largest trunk, my bag for a pillow. Mr. S. at the other end of the wagon, Dan on a blanket underneath, to get shelter from the heavy dew—the silent man & Jack on the ground near us with our mules—there was soon silence in the camp—This last night of wagon journeying went swiftly by—I was so much exhausted that any place to lay my head would have seemed a down pil- low almost—

3d The next thought I had was when Dan put his head under
the wagon cover, telling me breakfast was ready—It was
of the best the place afforded chickens—fresh eggs & corn
cakes—The women came to see me, overjoyed as they said
"dat de Lord let em see a white lady's face once more."
They had been here two years, most of the time alone—
clearing young master's place, One of them a light mulatto,
had an air of refinement which showed better "raising"—
She had been lady's maid in one of the numberless Southern "first families"—in the division of property at "ole master's" death, she fell to this son, and as she expressed it
"though I never worked hard a day in my life before, he
fetch me to this wilderness, an I ben in the field ever since,"
["]my children's all lef behind, they fell to Master's sister in
Alabamy, an I never heard from them since—If they was
here, I could work, but now I haint no heart left to do
anything—seems like"—I spoke to her of that land where
no partings come, with tears she answered—"Yes, mistress,
thank the Lord we'll have one home, and one Master there
forever." Except the cargo of slaves brought over in the
Wanderer nothing I had ever seen of slavery touched me
more. Those men were said to have belonged to the higher
classes in Africa—these had been accustomed to a life to-
tally different—I gave them my remnant of sugar and cake—
the first they had seen in two years they said—I was thankful when the time came to leave, for my sympathies were
painfully roused —and I knew how useless it was to feel
so—We had 25 miles yet to go—so, we pressed on, Mr Stone
going ahead as scout. Stopping at a cabin for water, we
heard loud sobbing and the voice of a young girl in expressions of agony—The old negro woman told us "Miss, Mary's
sweetheart was killed more nor four weeks ago at Vicksburg an she just heard of it now"—Sorrow everywhere, not
one place had we stopped, where war's marks could not be
seen—For every poor man who helps to make up "that human machine called a regiment" there may be sad ones at
home who watch and wait his coming—too often watching
in vain. "The brave General," or "the gallant Colonel" gains
all the honors of victory when it comes, if defeated, the

poor drink the bitterest dregs in the cup of suffering. War never seemed half so cruel or useless before–The prices of all the ordinary necessaries of life place them beyond the reach of the families of poor soldiers–and the rich care little for their wants. With domestics at from $2.50 to $4.00 per yd. flour from 50, to 75 $ per barrel. know little of comfort, paid as the men are only common soldiers wages. bare existence is all they seem to expect till the war is over. The groans of the taxed rich are loud and deep. The military holding complete sway know no rule but "might makes right–" About ten this morning we reached the Coldwater –the last point w[h]ere Confederate pickets are posted– There was an unusual number on the scare of "Yankees coming." When Mr. S. presented his pass, they di[s]puted its genuineness–looking back to the wagon very suspiciously–I saw there was trouble, and had vividly recalled an account of a Yankee lady arrested only a few days before I started, and "imprisoned on suspicion of being a spy" ["]in the lower part of the state." We waited quietly till Mr. S. by coolness and determination overcame their scruples– and the flat-boat was brought to our side of the stream. It had been sawed nearly apart–by some "raiders" not long before, and was not the most agreeable means of conveyance being partly under water–but, I went over first, then in small lots–our treasures–mules & all–"Getting through the lines" was at last accomplished. a formidable undertaking it had seemed, because so many things "might have been"–but, they were not for us–Ceasar carried no more exultant heart when the Rubicon was passed than beat in that rough wagon as we came to the cane-brake–for I felt that danger from one side was over–Gen. Ruggles friendly words of advice had often come over me–"Miss S. had better not only stop trying to get a pass, but stop thinking or talking of it, for she couldn't get through our lines now possibly." I had thought of the universal "we told you so" which would greet me on every hand if obliged to go back as so many had been. At the river we gained the first definite information about the Yankee raid–They were yesterday "in the bottom" on the only road through the cane-

brake⁴⁹—With our scouts ahead, the dumb man in the rear,
we went into the close muddy cart-path, scarcely wide
enough for our train, the canes growing high above the
wagon top, and as thick as even that rich soil could support—above them immense cotton-wood and gum trees
with festoons the most luxuriant vines hanging from their
branches. The morning was cloudy, a hotter place is hardly
concievable this side of where Dante journeyed in imagination. Musquitoes like misfortunes "come not singly but in
battalions["]—always ready for an attack. When we came to
impassable mud holes—the only alternative was to turn
into the cane, and tread down a new road—then the air
was filled with all manner of insects robbed of their home
so suddenly—All along the roadside were stray fleeces of
cotton—the remains of what had been sent clandestinely
to Memphis—generally under cover of the night—It was
concealed in the canes to prevent its being burned by the
Confederate government officers.—then carried to the Yankee
boats in small quantities—Even some army officers—who in
the beginning of the war, would "give their last dollar on
the altar of their country" had it was said recieved gold
from the hands of the detested Yankees—though their
touch was thought such defilement—except through that
incorruptible medium. These vast thickets have been the
hiding-place of runaway negroes ever since the country was
settled—since the war deserters from the army have taken
their places. Strange turning of Fortune's wheel—the for-
mer slaves are now freeing themselves by hundreds—a tyr-
anny not much exceeded by slavery rules those who were
once masters—No poor man can escape conscription except by concealment—When about five miles along—on this
way—we came to the first large clearing—Judge G's plantation—he told us we were in danger any minute of being
overtaken by a party—which rode past his house the day
before—coming from the river on a foraging expedition—
He expected a call on their return. The intense heat, and
occasional halts to cut down trees we had run against—the
constant fear of losing our motive powers, and being compelled to plod out on foot as many a luckless one has done

—who chanced to be met by a "raid"—all combined to make this a "long drawn out" day of misery—But "despair is never quite despair." "Nil desperandum" was my motto in starting and now—the journey was almost over in distance at least—Once, as a bear jumped across the path, I thought we were doomed—but—Bruin was not after us at all—Jack and I kept up conversation briskly—we being left in the rear—with directions to hide in the canes if we heard many horses coming together—which I had not a doubt he would do—This would leave me literally to "go it alone"— The poetry which Saxe wrote sounds very well, when he tells us that in the game of life as in euchre, we may hold the best cards, "Yet, the game may be lost, with all these for your own, Unless you've the courage to "go it alone["]" —I had nothing left but a Jack, and that was a poor dependence, with which to "follow suit" if Yankees led—under these circumstances—However I had not even the privilege of looking like poor renowned Lot's wife—who is now shown to travelers still looking back—"in status quo"—The canes were too dense and high to see many yards behind or before us—We and our mules were walking by faith—through one of the lighter places, a large buck dashed across our path—not even giving us a look—By three—the air began to grow heavier, and darker—we could hardly get a glimpse of the sky through the tall trees—but, knew well that a thunder storm was coming soon—Dan was sleeping heavily in the front of the wagon, having a high fever after a chill— He had rode back—being unable to keep on his mule any longer—which added nothing to the cheerfulness of the hour—The thunder and lightning in half an hour were incessant, We could see the tree tops twisted about by the fury of the wind, far above us—and soon down came the rain in torrents—After much urging Dan changed places with me, for my seat had a cover—This was our first experience of bad weather—"Some days must be dark and dreary" we all know—All things considered, I thought it would be hard to imagine a much darker or drearier time, but, when one is thoroughly wet, there is a quiet assurance in the fact that we have seen the worst "the fates can do"—and we set-

tle down determined to make the best of it—let what will
come—one soon learns that "to bear is to conquer our
fate"—At home, even, the grandeur of this form of nature's
works—being always to me more of terror than enjoyment—
for twice I have felt the shock of its striking very near—It
was an indescribable relief, when we came to an open space
—the storm had not lessened, but, we seemed to have
emerged from a dark prison—and could see a few rods
ahead—We came to a cabin, and being captain pro-tem, I
ordered a halt—as we rode up—found Mr. S. had been anxiously waiting for us, and was mounting his horse to go
back, fearing something had happened—We waded over
shoes—to get into the house—where were a dozen people—
the men smoking and drinking the women "dipping snuff"
in which they urged me to join—telling me I "missed a
mighty heap" They asked Mr. S. if "his 'oman never dipped
sure"—and stared incredulously when he told them I never
did. We heard graphic accounts of what "the Yankees done
here["]—about sun up yesterday—the poor "lady of the
manor" summing up by saying "they never lef nary thing
with legs on the place ceptin us"—Their panacea for all the
woes of Southern women snuff was left—and I could not
but think what a double energy would be added to the
punches with those althea sticks in their broad mouths—if
they only knew that one of the same Yankee nation was
face to face with them—but,—Mr. Stone did the talking—
till we concluded that it was useless to wait for the rain to
be over—It was nearly six, and we had four miles of black
mud to plod through—yet—and what mud—when I remon-
strated with Jack for so unmercifully whipping the jaded
mules—his answer was—"Mistis if I jes lets em stop oncet
here, dey'll be standin here till Gabriel comes down—dey
musn't know day kin stop"—["]dat's de only way to do wid
mules"—Mr. S. would ride up occasionally and comfort me
by saying he knew every stump now we were almost there
—We passed one fine plantation with every building burnt—
the effect of a last winter's raid—At dark our six day's
journey ended in a cordial welcome at Mr. Stone's house—
Wet, hungry, worn out—but—with a heart overflowing

102

with gratitude to that Hand which "thus far had led me
on["]–feeling as says the old Moravian hymn,

> Through waves, through clouds and storms,
> He gently clears thy way,
> Wait thou His time, so shall the night,
> Soon end in joyous day.–

This night was to me what I imagine the home of a sailor
is, when he has just escaped shipwreck. I heard the rain on
the roof, swarms of musquitoes outside the bar, I knew
there were sharp flashes of lightning, and heavy peals of
thunder, but felt protected from them–all sheltered once
more–It was late on Sunday morning before I awoke–already the neighbors were gathering in from the country
round–to talk over the war news, and detail their exploits
with Yankees–I soon saw that there was very little devotion to the Confederacy, perhaps because a Yankee market
was too accessible. "The bottom" as it is called, is a tract of
very rich land formed entirely from overflows of the Mississippi–It produces immense crops of corn & cotton, chills
& musquitoes–is owned almost entirely by planters living
elsewhere, and managed by overseers whose only ambition
is to "make a big crop"–no matter by what means. Since
the Yankee raids–most of the "hands" are gone–have
either been carried "into the hills" for safe keeping, or have
taken themselves into a free country–Laugh as they may at
the Emancipation Proclamation–it seems to me slavery is
doomed–Some of the people spoke of their "protection
papers"–got in Memphis by taking the oath–All com-
plained bitterly at the neglect of their own government[50]–
Scarcely any horses or mules were to be found they said–
either one or the other side had taken them. One gent, a
member of the last Confed. Congress came on the back of
a worn out mule–which he had borrowed from a neighbor
–before the war he was rich–now he had neither house–
servant or horse. Yet I shall long remember his kindness
in offering to give me a letter of introduction to Judge
Venable who had tried the principal cases of political affairs
in Memphis since it had been "taken"–["]We're about gone

up"–was the expression of to one–to which no one seemed
inclined to make any comment–With their business at a
stand–no churches–or schools–they seemed only to wish
for peace–It was hard to understand what their enjoy-
ments could ever be–beyond the bare accumulation of
money–carriages were unknown there–as they would be
useless most of the year–Vegetation was grand in variety as
well as size–Vines running to the tops of tall trees–sometimes a few feet from the trunk going up for a hundred feet
perfectly straight having started with the young tree long
years ago–There was an incessant chattering of paroquettes
–somewhat after the style in which "they say a woman's
right's convention is carried on["]–The birds being green
are invisible when among the branches–they are very de-
structive in a corn field–Walking here was impossible even
with my home-made leather shoes–equal to any genuine
"brogans".[51] so a week passed away very quietly–except the
constant occupation of brushing off the largest musquitoes
I ever saw–I found little to do but rest–The story of my
pounding about in the wagon was told in sundry and various black spots on my person–as well as a general stiffness
and disinclination to move–Mrs. Stone did all in her power
to make my stay pleasant. Here, all were told I was going to
Memphis–how much more they surmised–mattered not.

August 12th–Monday morning–A week of absolute quiet has
　　restored my desire to be "moving on"–towards my jour-
　　ney's end–This is still quite a long way off–bidding my kind
　　hostess and family "good bye"–I started again–this time in
　　a one horse wagon–Jack for driver–my 'chair for a seat–
　　Dan with my trunks and Mr. Stone following us–we had
　　seven miles to ride to the river where we hoped to get a
　　boat–going to Memphis. Not a quarter of a mile from the
　　house, Jack drove into a mud-hole–into which the wheels
　　on my side sank indefinitely–I perched on a high chair
　　with nothing to hold by–being "unexpectedly called on"
　　like so many patriotic orators–out went chair and its occu-
　　pant between the wheels–A sudden stopping of the horse
　　prevented more serious trouble, or my friend's predictions

about my reaching the North would probably have been
verified, and my inglorious career ended here. Though less
agreeable, falling in the mud so far as safety goes, is far
preferable to a firmer landing-place – Mr. Stone came hurrying up to me insisting on my being hurt, and going back –
but, after walking a few steps – I found no injury – and was
soon reseated this time not ambitious for a high place, I sat
on the bottom of the wagon – We saw an enormous water
mocassin gliding away from the bank of a creek we crossed
–apparently in great fear of us – The plantations through
which we passed were all overgrown with weeds – one on
which the ordinary crop was 1000 bales of cotton, & corn
in proportion had not a negro at work – Even the plantation road was so hidden – we could hardly find it – There
was only silence and desolation, till we came in sight of the
Father of Waters – this was my first view – and rather small
it looked to me – compared with my ideas of it. Half a mile
farther along the levee, brought us to a place opposite
Island No. 40 or Buck Island which was my destination –
An old bachelor from Boston originally was the major
domo – We were just going into his house, when we saw
the boatman landing – Mr. S. soon told him that I wanted
to be carried over to his house on the Island and wait for a
boat. Down the almost perpendicular bank I clambered,
with the help of Mr. S. & Dan both – my trunks followed,
and we were all deposited in the little leaky "skiff" – This
seemed more like "flying from ills we have" &tc than anything before on the journey When Mr. S. & Dan gave me
the farewell grasp of hands – and Jack his not less hearty
one, I left all behind of whom I had ever heard – They had
been to me "friends in need" such as can not soon be forgotten – The sun was at noon-day height – and scorching
heat – Our ride was short, fortunately, we landed at the
steep bank & ploughed up through the hot sand to the
house – found a cabin – with one room – occupied by a
squalid woman & 6 children – This was the only place of
shelter on the island. Dinner was prepared, but – my appe-
tite failed – the water was lukewarm, just as it was dipped
up from the river – The evening passed in hearing details of

a visit they had from a band of Southern guerrillas ten days before—who came across from the "main shore"—robbed them in broad daylight of all the money & clothing they could find —& most of their scanty hard earned stock of provisions—They were infuriated by finding the oath of allegiance to the U.S.—which the man had in his trunk—In reality, they were deserters from Gen. Chalmer's army, and men or brutes rather well known to both this man & his wife for years—the man was away—the band left—telling his wife they would come back & get him soon. Daylight faded away—& no boat came—A sleeping place was improvised for me, on the floor of what was called a piazza—a few boards overhead—no sides or front—This was better than sharing a room with 8 others a small one at that—A large black dog lay by me—I was in no mood for sleep—the bright moonlight was the only ray of comfort—Something would move, & I could see stealthy guerrillas on every side—two contrabands were stalking around like black ghosts till after midnight—They had been left by one gunboat and were watching for another—to get away—Robinson Crusoe seemed truer than ever to me—though I had not read it for years—it came fresh to my memory—The river lay sleeping so quietly below—but, even its calmness did not soothe me—Every faculty but reason was wide awake. Two boats came puffing round the bend, and passed on—How my thoughts followed them up many a mile in the river's course, to where my only brother I supposed was still living—After the birds had all sung their good night—& the insects grown more subdued in their music—there was a stillness like death brooding over everything—the pale stars looked down so tenderly—that one's thoughts could not but turn to Him whose handiwork are both they—and poor trembling mortals—'Tis said, that "silence is vocal if we listen well"—when the first dawning of morning light came, I had not for an instant ceased to lend a listening ear, never did I more heartily "hail the glorious morn"—At sunrise on the high bank—I watched the beautiful painting of every object—The country being level, wants the grandeur of more varied scenery—but it has a quiet majesty at

this hour–beyond description. While there alone, I first
saw the old flag–the dear old Stars And Stripes. It looked
to me now like the protecting arm of a father stretched out
to me–the tears fell thick and fast as it passed on–and my
signal was unheeded. I had heard that flag called by every
derisive name, seen another for 2 years waving over a distracted country–now, my prayers were answered–and my
love for it was stronger than I knew before–Now from the
rising place of this grand river in the far Northern Lake, to
its last wave as it enters the Gulf, there floats on its bosom
no other flag than the old Star Spangled Banner–enough
in that thought to swell every American's heart–All day
boats were passing up and down, not one of them even
slackening their speed for my white signal. Gen. Chalmer's
forces had not long before fired on one [of] them from the
landing near there–Commerce, which in return was soon
after burnt–and strict orders were given from head-quarters
that nothing but a gun-boat should stop there–the levee
afforded fine protection for sharp shooters–who could take
off the pilots.–Of this Mr. S knew nothing when I came
there–he thinking boats stopped as they had before–very
often–Here was a new dilemma–which grew into mighty
proportions as night came on–With river water to drink,
miserable food to eat, and feeling sensibly the general effect
of my yesterday's fall from the wagon–added to the hope-
lessness of escape for some time–this was a gloomy day
enough–and a few more drops were added to what I thought
my full bucket of misery, in the shape of a thunder storm
which drove me into "the room" coming up about bed-
time–There was no lack of air–for the logs were not close
enough together for that–nor rain–either–but–the night
wore away–Wednesday morning was cooler–somewhat–I
walked to the bank again–this time almost despairing.
There was just breeze enough to rustle the leaves of the
cotton-wood trees, with a sound like gentle rain–the creeping mimosa coming up in the sand was waiting the sun's
rays to unfold its delicate leaves and flowers–Waiting till
the sun had for an hour been shining, I went back–to
spend a restless uncomfortable day–feeling much like a

prisoner condemned without a trial—When the hot sun
was down again—I went to the farther end of the island
about half a mile—with the oldest daughter of 14 yrs. Dark
purple clouds were piled up in the distance and zig-zag
lightning flashed across them—far back seemed like a sheet
of flame flickering but never dying out—It was awfully
grand—the fear of its coming nearer deprived me of all enjoyment—and I thought too of another night in that room
with the whole family—The clouds gradually sank away—
that fear was gone—Some good angel must have been at
my side just then telling me that this was an omen for me
—for a thought came to me—that in my trunk were some
pieces of red white & blue silk—remnants of a Union flag—
made for the last rally before the war in Columbus—Hurrying back—I made as large a flag as I could with them, cut
paper stars out of a blank leaf in my note-book—and soon
had a Star spangld—though small sized—national emblem—
With a cotton-wood stick for staff, it was tied on—the stars
down—in token of distress—It was laid under my scanty
pillow, and when I fell asleep—it was with a firm conviction, that These darkest days—wait till to-morrow—would
all have passed away—and I be released from Buck Island.
The prisoners on both sides who have dragged out long
weary months often of unjust confinement were often in
my mind in these three days for this was my first experience of a feeling of confinement in close quarters—Of the
suffering among Southern men—I have heard stories without end, and often I could not but believe without even
the slim "founded on fact" of novel title pages.—Of Southern prisons I have seen nothing, except the small number
in Columbus—& them only at the windows. At best—the
loss of liberty is a bitter thing—without useless severity on
either side—That night I slept soundly—The morning sun
woke me—for nothing came between me and its first beams
—Breakfast was here only an apology for eating, like all the
other meals with me, as too much of the "peck" we are all
said to have as our alloted portion of dirt in this life—was
apparent. An hour passed—two, three—no boat—but, before noon we heard a slow puffing coming up—The family

went to the bank with me—my trunks having gone early—
My little flag was flung to the breeze—I could see the pilot
with his glass watching—what minutes of suspense those
were—had it not been for my firm faith in my poor little
"Stars & Stripes"—I should have been hopeless of success—
but it came for the bell struck twice—the signal to stop—
The sound thrilled through my ears—and overpowered me
—for it told me—my task was done. It was a welcome back
to my native land—With trembling hand, and dim eyes—I
bade good-bye to the poor woman and her miserable children—and with my trunks embarked once more in the
"skiff"—to go out into the middle of the river a short—but
not very safe adventure, being nearly drawn under the boat
—as we came "alongside" The decks were crowded with fur-
loughed men and officers coming from Vicksburg, With
the help of some strong arms—I mounted from the top
of my trunk—to the boat's side—in a few minutes we were
off—The old captain took me to the pilot-house—where he
said that although I did not realize it—the greatest danger
in my trip had just passed—He had screamed—"don't bring
her out"—which we on shore did not understand—and
he said every-body expected to see us swamped in the current—after "perils by land"—this last "peril by water" had
seemed less to me—than many others—for I could see the
goal—Words poorly express the feeling of security—as I sat
looking out on the "dangers passed"—once more there was
over me the emblem of a strong government—not the flag
of a distracted anarchy—where confusion ruled and reigned
—in the struggle for power—That land I had loved—and
not less in her sorrow—with pity for the blindness which
caused her ruin—and unchanging affection for my friends.
Now for the first time I began to hear the Union side of
"the Rebellion" a new word to me—New name for "this
glorious struggle for our freedom" on which so many
changes had been rung. Officers were anxious to learn
what little I could tell them of things in general—in Dixie
land—An hour's conversation showed me there was a great
difference in the bitterness of the two sides not less determination to succeed—no one seemed to question the

final result—Our boat was named The Moderator, and proved herself worthy the title—for we dragged along—all impatient to reach Memphis—One Lieut—was kind enough to share his crackers and cheese with me—else though our trip was slow, mine must have been a fast—One and another—talked of their pleasure in anticipation—of a mother & sisters to greet them after so long absence, of "somebody and her baby" who have missed me at home I know —one said ["]I'm going home with one arm less—but my right one is left—and that belongs to my country yet, boys"—My friend of the lunch told me [he] was born in a slave state—had always owned them, but, said he, "they and all I have shall go, before this government shall suffer at the hands of rebels while I can do anything however small to sustain it"—I had look on "that picture"—now this was the other—["]One story is good till another is told"— always—The scenery was monotonous enough—"the most noticeable feature["] being—the lack of anything to notice—Sandy banks, with drift-wood and often large trees left by the overflows high and dry on them, with a low country behind them—were the unvarying outline of the view. here & there was the skeleton of some wrecked boat —some had been burned during the war, and their blackened ribs tell the dark tale—many more have gone out of sight forever—snagged and sunk. We had but 30 miles to get to Memphis—but it took us 8 hours. The river was very low, and the dark mischievous looking snags were scattered all along its course. Sometimes we felt the ominous shaking and dragging which says so plainly "sure aground"—but we were soon off—our pilot being like the one who on being asked if he knew where the snags were, replied "No, but I know where they ain't, and that's where I go"—["]generally"—He showed the marks of blood on the posts of his room, where his predecessor had been shot by guerillas on the shore only 6 weeks before, and said he would not have dared stop for me, but that he knew the man on that island was a genuine Union man—finding some Minnesota troops on board, I used the pilot's bed for a writing desk, and wrote a short letter to Channing.

The Col. was going directly to St. Paul, but could only understand German, which I could not speak—only to thank him—At quite a late hour in the afternoon, we edged our way to the wharf in Mempis—among the crowd of boats—The kind old captain would take only my thanks for his trouble, giving me a caution not to inform any one on what boat I came—as his stopping against orders—though he said you may thank the pilot for it not me—so, to the last day I live shall I be grateful to him—He told me—"twas nothing—I saw a woman in trouble, your flag showed you knew how to tell it to a sailor—an you'll never ask help from them and not get it—if they all feel as I do about women"—I took a carriage and drove to the Gayoso House —the best hotel—I knew. The blond clerk refused me a room, saying "he could not give one to a lady coming alone"—My letters of introduction came in play, though he only looked at the outsides—I was soon well cared for—drove to Dr. Stedman's house to deliver the one from Dr. Lyon—He returned with me to the hotel, next morning kindly came to take me to the Bank and Provost Marshal's office—to take the oath &tc—which we found was needless trouble—as those orders had been withdrawn requiring that—How strange it was to see negro soldiers on guard in full uniform—Yankee papers—too, were of the greatest interest of all to me—"guessing" so differently from the "reckonings" I had heard—Memphis was full of shoulder-strapped men and their families. In the parlor during the morning I formed a very pleasant acquaintance of a Capt. Smith & his pretty young wife & baby going directly to Cincinnati. The day was intolerably hot—and Memphis in anything but a cleanly condition—we were glad to leave at 4 P.M.— the boat was crowded, we were kept an hour waiting, lying in the low water—with the sun reflected from the steep bank upon us—The sight of a sick soldier on the floor made our own discomforts seem very slight—as he panted for breath—while his poor worn out mother fanned him constantly—refusing to let any one take her place—though he did not know her—Had we not been too warm for so much exertion, what a shout would have gone forth from

that fanning crowd, as we pushed off, and felt a slight
breeze giving us new life—We had one Gen. Cols. & Capts.
without number as passengers—crowded in the cabins, we
were early "on the retired list"—scarcely in our rooms—
before the cry—"a man overboard"—rung out on our end
of the boat—Of course there was a rush of both men and
women—everyone of the last firmly convinced that it was
her own and only dearly beloved—if that same happened
to be out of sight just at the minute—There were scream-
ings and sobbings unutterable—in the star-light we could
see his head bobbing up and down—and hear his cry "help,
O help,["] which was growing fainter—The small boat was
instantly lowered, and the man saved just as he was the
third time going down. There was a subsiding of sympathy, as well as persons "en deshabile" when we found it was
a drunken gun-boat man—who had fallen over the lower
guards—The night was cool, after my inquisitive companion
had found out enough to satisfy her of my past and future,
sleep was refreshing—and unbroken till next morning—By
sunrise, I was on the upper deck, with many others—catching a breath of air while we could—Saw here—a Godey for
the first time in over three years.[52] Harper's Illustrated
looked like gems of art after seeing the attempt made in
Richmond to imitate it in war scenes & portraits—As it
became known that I was just "coming out of the wilderness" of secession—other things were brought me—as curi-
osities—The first "cartes-de-visite" I had seen were among
them—I saw that if "the grass grown streets" were a verity
in Yankeedom—there had not been stupor everywhere.
One woman amused me by asking whar did yer clothes
come from—I thought they hedn't got any down South.
One poor sad woman we were told, was returning from a
trip to Vicksburg—where she went to see a sick son, whom
with her husband she had found dead—the son only the
morning of her arrival—and she without a dollar to get
back home—This want was supplied by a contribution
among the passengers—but—who could fill the aching void
of her heart—Wisconsin was her home—to which she was
going alone—and poor—It has seemed to me strange in all

this war, that so many pass along as though they did not
know there was sorrow every-where–in the whole land–
for it has been before my eyes everywhere–and "over the
lines" there is enough call for sympathy surely–We were
a tired company throughout, and crowded to the last extremity–Cairo–justly the dread of travelers–was welcomed
–for it brought a change–As the bells were ringing for
church on Sunday morning we landed there–and toiled up
that steep bank to a wretched hotel–swarming with flies,
and negroes–Admiral Porter's flag ship passed soon after,
& a salute was fired from all the boats–a strange mixture of
"the pomp and circumstance of war"–with the calls to hear
"the gospel of peace"–We were promised only three hours
detention here, but, it grew to six as is the almost daily experience–with neither provision for one's comfort, or any
disposition to make up in courtesy what sometimes supplies
the place of more solid material–Our train was crowded–
moved slowly–and we reached Odin two hours after the
Cincinnati train had left–passengers for St. Louis as well–
Six of us occupied the ticket office–and three children. All
the remaining space was "pre-empted" by musquitoes–
who must have been on short rations for some time–The
platform outside was covered with soldiers sleeping soundly
–and snoring prodigiously–Were it not for the "what's the
use of sighing" philosophy–such a night would exhaust
one's patience–but–like every other night it had a morning–we filed out taking our turns at the tin basins and
well-used towels–and crowded to breakfast–which was the
best part of our stay here–to our host be all the honor as
he did his best–At ten the Cinn. train came–we were "all
aboard" and off in ["]double quick" time–On our way
nothing occurred to call even a faint smile forth–save the
lively demonstration of spirit from a car-load of "gun-boat
men"–in chastising a "copperhead"–a new and entirely
unintelligible term to me[53]–While we were getting water–
they beat him unmercifully. Whatever sin the word im-
plies, I thought must have beaten out–if blows could produce regeneration. Their good bye salutation was–"What
do you think of old Abe's men now?" The country had a

look of peculiar freshness–after a heavy rain–unlike anything South–the trees full of fruit–and sweeter than all to
me were the brooks as we whizzed by–living in a level
country we never saw them–The only thing which reminded us of war, was a notice "There are positively no
rebels on this road now" at one of the stations–It had
been the scene of Gen. Morgan's brilliant exploits–which
ended so ingloriously a short time before.[54]At 2½ on Tuesday morning we reached Cinn, tried 4 hotels before we
found "rest for the weary"–"all full" everywhere–we were
placed in the fourth story, but, glad of sleep anywhere–At
a late hour we breakfasted–parted with promises to write
and continue an acquaintance–which I had found so pleasant–Sent a note to my cousin's husbands Messrs. Barker &
Finsey who in a few minutes answered in person–& took
me to Mr. Barker's house–Cousin Anto. not having seen
me since I was a child–did not recognize me at first but it
soon became a cordial greeting, and a pressing invitation to
wait a week & go to New York in company with her–instead of hurrying on next day–I concluded to do so–and
passed ten days delightfully there. Once more the sounds
and sights of a city were around me–instead of spinning
wheels–I heard the whistles of steam engines the hammers
of workmen building on every side–saw morning papers–
street cars–things alive again–and seeing them forces the
contrast of the past few years–in a country at war "a game
which were the nations wise they would not play at." It
was strangest of all to realize that there was no danger in
the full expression of an honest opinion whatever it be–
After so long seeing the question of Slavery "tabooed"–
being compelled to keep silence often when I longed to
express sympathy for suffering, because it would do injury
–both to myself and others–who were not independent
the plain outspoken resolution to "conquer or die" was
not at all of the "nor to the knife & the knife to the hilt"
school–With personal sympathies hard to overcome, I
could not join in the spirit of conquest–for I had known
too well what it cost the conquered–and felt too much for
and with them–We had other and more pleasant subjects

for our thoughts and words, as Southbridge memories
were revived–Frances & I talking over childish days–and
the years between then and now. Hers had been passed in
her own quiet home–mine far differently.

August 27th Almost a month from the day of my starting–we
left Cinc. for New York It will ever have pleasant memories
to me–for that visit We passed Camp Denison, which
looked like a clean village–uniformly built, now used for
sick soldiers. A sweet familiar perfume came to me–long
forgotten–new made hay–in the rich meadows beside the
track–Just at evening we came to Columbus–where are
Gen. Morgan's present headquarters at the Penitentiary–
and with only a short stop–on to Cleveland, where we
took the Lake Shore road–for the night. tried for the first
time a sleeping car–& like it much–Next morning we
passed through the beautiful Mohawk Valley–beautiful
everywhere. It seems almost sacrilege to rush through natural pictures in an Express train–meant only for the hurry
of business. On we rushed, leaving the pretty river–with
its green banks–and quiet villages–at nine were in Albany
–where cousin Anto. Barker & I parted–she going on the
Western road towards Boston–I–down the Hudson River
Road to New York–At every point on this road are "things
of beauty"–either from the hand of Nature's God, or the
lesser works of man–In five hours our train was in the
noise and bustle of New York–with everybody "moving
on"–and everything in the streets pushing and being pushed
out of the way–of somebody–I was entirely overcome by
the frightened looks of a tall Vermonter & his two verdant
sisters–who asked me–if I could tell them where to hire a
team to carry them to Brooklyn–On telling them that was
my stopping place–they said less go 'long with her–but as
we came near Broadway–the poor fellow said be you sure
this is the road–every thing I said seemed to rouse his fears
the worse–& his sisters in their new dresses looked utterly
bewildered–This was their first sight of a live city–they
had come to visit a cousin–some of the country cousins
we read of–They followed me closely–across the river–&

took the same street car–he telling the ferryman & conductor both–he paid once up yender–when their "fare sir"
came–They stopped at Smith St–hand in hand–I saw
them last going to hunt up relations who would wish them
back in Vermont–most likely–Found the house shut
up–at 3 Carroll Park–but, soon got the key next door–In
port again–after this tedious journey–in which though a
"lone woman"–I had found friends and help every-where–
In no other than my native land would this have been possible. Most devoutly I thank God that He has protected
me through so many dangers–once more to see "the land
of the free"–soon I hope to grasp the hand of my uncle &
his family–then my only brother–As I sit–this morning–
thinking over all three years since I was last here–I seem to
have been living in another world–and slowly traveled
back to this–For what–

To the Editor of the St. Paul Pioneer:

There is something so noble and Christ like in the following that I beg you to give it a place in your Sunday morning issue. I would have it learned by Sunday School children, and read by every one in the land. From the Atlantic Monthly.

THE BLUE AND THE GRAY.*

By the flow of the inland river,
    Whence the fleets of iron have fled,
Where the blades of the grave-grass quiver,
    Asleep are the ranks of the dead ;—
        Under the sod and the dew,
            Waiting the judgment day ;
        Under the one, the Blue ;
            Under the other, the Gray.

These in the robings of glory,
    Those in the gloom of defeat,
All with the battle-blood gory,
    In the dusk of eternity meet ;
        Under the sod and the dew,
            Waiting the judgment day ;
        Under the laurel, the Blue ;
            Under the willow, the Gray.

From the silence of sorrowful hours
    The desolate mourners go,
Lovingly laden with flowers
    Alike for the friend and the foe ;—
        Under the sod and the dew,
            Waiting the judgement day ;
        Broidered with gold, the Blue ;
            Mellowed with gold, the Gray.

So when Summer calleth,
    On forest and field of grain
With an equal murmur falleth
    The cooling drip of the rain ;
        Under the sod and the dew,
            Waiting the judgement day ;
        Wet with the rain, the Blue ;
            Wet with the rain, the Gray.

Sadly, but not with upbraiding,
    The generous deed was done ;
In the storm of the years that are fading,
    No braver battle was won ;
        Under the sod and the dew,
            Waiting the judgement day ;
        Under the blossoms, the Blue,
            Under the garlands, the Gray.

No more shall the war-cry sever,
    Or the winding rivers be red ;
They banish our anger forever
    When they laurel the graves of our dead !
        Under the sod and the dew,
            Waiting the judgement day ;
        Love and tears for the Blue,
            Tears and love for the Gray.

"The women of Columbus, Mississippi, animated by nobler sentiments than are many of their sisters, have shown themselves impartial in their offerings made to the memory of the dead. They strewed flowers alike on the graves of the Confederate and of the National soldiers." —New York Tribune.

The final manuscript page of Caroline Seabury's diary, including a newspaper clipping of a letter to the editor of the *St. Paul Pioneer.* Included in the clipping is the poem "The Blue and the Gray," originally published in *The Atlantic Monthly.* Courtesy of the Minnesota Historical Society.

A sketch made by Caroline Seabury of the group of wagons and horses led by Mr. Stone in which she escaped through Confederate lines in August 1863. Courtesy of the Minnesota Historical Society.

A clipping lampooning Confederate President Jefferson Davis, who was said to have tried to escape at the end of the Civil War by posing as a woman. This clipping was pasted onto the back pages of the diary. Courtesy of the Minnesota Historical Society.

The Life of Lincoln, Written by Himself.

GEORGETOWN, D. C., April 27, 1865.— As everything connected with the history of our martyr President is of intense interest I send you a brief record which illustrates his singular modesty as a man. When, in 1858, I commenced my labors on the work known as the "Dictionary of Congress," I forwarded to every ex-member of Congress whose residence I could ascertain a circular asking each person for information as to the date and place of his birth, the character of his education, his profession or occupation, and a list of any public positions he may have filled. These simple facts were all I wanted, and in looking over the thousands of replies that have been sent me since it is truly remarkable to find that men of the greatest ability have invariably told a direct and brief story, thereby preserving their innate modesty and writing nothing to compromise their dignity. The reply which I received from Mr. Lincoln was singularly brief, and yet comprehensive, and you may well imagine is now highly valued by me, with other friendly letters, by the same hand, as a memento of one who possessed all the "degrees of sovereign honor," as elucidated by Lord Bacon; and who, like Regulus and the two Decii, sacrificed his life for the good of his country. The record in question is as follows:—

Born February 12, 1809, in Hardin county, Kentucky.
Education defective.
Profession, a lawyer.
Have been a captain of volunteers in the Black Hawk war.
Post master at a very small office.
Four times a member of the Illinois Legislature.
And was a member of the lower House of Congress.

Yours, &c.,
A. LINCOLN.

The Finest Speech Ever Made

The *Westminister Review* pronounces Abraham Lincoln's Gettysburg speech the finest speech that ever fell from human lips. In view of this fact, and that it is even more pertinent than it ever was, we need make no apology for republishing it, especially as it will but little occupy space. We give it below:

"Four score and seven years ago our fathers brought forth upon this continent a new nation, conceived in liberty and dedicated to the proposition that all men are created equal. Now we are engaged in a civil war, testing whether that nation, or any nation conceived or dedicated, can long endure. We are met on a great battle field of that war. We are met to dedicate a portion of it as the final resting place of those who here gave their lives that that nation might live. It is altogether fitting and proper that we should do this.

But in a large sense we cannot consecrate, we cannot hallow this ground. The brave men, living and dead, who struggled here, have consecrated it far above our power to add or detract. The world will little note nor long remember what we say here, but it can never forget what they did here. It is for us, the living, rather to be dedicated to the unfinished work that they have thus far so nobly carried on. It is rather for us to be here dedicated to the great task remaining before us—that from these honored dead we take increased devotion to the cause for which they here gave the last full measure of devotion—that we here highly resolve that the dead shall have not died in vain—that the nation shall, under God, have a new birth of freedom, and that the government of the people, by the people, and for the people shall not perish from the earth."

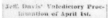

Jeff. Davis' Valedictory Proclamation of April 1st.

WHEREAS, In the course of inhuman Yankee events, the capital of the Confederate States of America no longer affords an eligible and healthy residence for the members of the present Cabinet, nor to speak of the Chief Magistrate himself, the Vice President, and the members of the two congressional bodies. I do therefore, by virtue of the power vested in my two heels, proclaim my intention to travel hitherto in company with all the officers of the Confederate States Government, and to take up such agreeable quarters as may yet be *treated* unto me.

To such persons as are in array against the Confederate States of America, I hereby tender absolute amnesty, on condition that they forthwith desist from annoying our patriotic population.

Under the circumstances, slavery had better be abolished.

The capital of the Confederacy will henceforward be found "up a stump," on the picturesque banks of the celebrated "Last Ditch."

...

Major General Grant, of the U. S. A., will please see that they get their cotton.

All persons having claims against this government will please present them to A. Lincoln, Richmond, by whom all such accounts will be most cheerfully audited.

It is not altogether improbable that the glorious experiment of a slaveholders' confederacy may yet prove a delusion and a snare. I have often thought so. So has General Lee, who has lately been fighting mostly for his last year's salary. The Confederate Treasury being light, I think I will take it in my valise. General Lee thinks that we have a good opening before us, and that we have seen the last of this fratricidal war. I hope so. Stephens thinks peace more assured than ever.

If the United States persists in refusing to recognize the confederacy, on my return I shall again urge the arming of the negroes.

Office-seekers are respectfully requested to cease their importunities. Fellow citizens farewell.

J. DAVIS,
President Confederate States of America.
Done at Richmond, April 1.

Photographs and newspaper clippings relating to Abraham Lincoln and Jefferson Davis, pasted by Caroline Seabury onto her diary's back pages. Courtesy of the Minnesota Historical Society.

Passes issued to Caroline Seabury in October 1862, *top*, and in July 1863, *bottom*, to pass through Confederate lines within Lowndes County, Mississippi. Also, a five-cent Confederate note, *center*, issued in Columbus, Mississippi on March 1, 1862. These memorabilia were pasted onto a back page in Caroline Seabury's diary. Courtesy of the Minnesota Historical Society.

Notes
Bibliography
Index

Notes

❦

Introduction

1. Traditionally, a diary has been viewed as a brief day-to-day record of events, while a journal has been viewed as a lengthy, introspective personal narrative. My research on unpublished diaries/journals written by nineteenth-century midwestern American women has shown that there is no clear dividing line between the two forms. Thus, for the purposes of this study I use the terms *diary* and *journal* interchangeably to characterize the text which Caroline Seabury wrote.

2. As Nancy Cott notes, schoolteaching became more important for women as family-centered production gave way to market-centered production and a new emphasis on the individual as wage earner. Women's education was to be utilitarian, with service to others as a woman's ultimate goal. All-female schools were established as a means of training future teachers (98ff).

Nancy Woloch observes that by 1850, one out of five Massachusetts women had taught at some point in her life (130). By 1860 one-fourth of the nation's teachers were women, and almost four-fifths of Massachusetts's teachers were women (129).

Nancy Hoffman's study of women teachers reveals that between 1840 and 1860 the number of female teachers in the United States tripled to make up approximately 80 percent of the elementary school teaching force (4). According to Hoffman, three social changes helped make teaching a growing profession for women: industrialization, immigration, and urbanization (8). Many women viewed teaching as preferable to working as a seamstress, domestic, or factory worker because teaching was genteel, permitted travel, and provided some independent income and economic security (3).

3. The art of traditional patchwork quilting involves the assembling and sewing of pieces of fabric that have been carefully cut and arranged into intricate geometric designs.

Elaine Showalter's article, "Piecing and Writing," has been especially useful to me as I have formulated my ideas about women's diary writing and as I have developed my own approach to studying women's lives and works. As Showalter puts it, "A knowledge of piecing, the technique of assembling fragments into an intricate and ingenious design, can provide the contexts

123

in which we can interpret and understand the forms, meanings, and narrative traditions of American women's writing" (227).

Women's diaries, like women's quilts, create patterns that tell stories about their lives. Both rely on their creator's powers of selection and her strategies of design. According to Showalter, piecing is "an art of scarcity, ingenuity, conservation, and order," not a repetitious, unoriginal recombining of certain kinds of design. Women's diaries also exhibit these characteristics.

4. Margo Culley analyzes the diary as a carefully wrought verbal construct in which the processes of selection and arrangement of detail play a central role (*Day at a Time* 10). Like Culley, Rebecca Hogan views the diary as a finely shaped entity which can serve as a "silent interlocutor" of a dialogue between parts of a self ("Diarists" 10). In speaking of women's diaries, Judy Lensink notes that, within any given diary, "a coherent world formed by the writer's perceptions does exist: populated by reappearing characters; mappable, even if only the size of a household" (382). Like me, Lensink finds the metaphor of piecing a quilt appropriate to the creation of a diary. These scholars' works have been particularly helpful to me as I have analyzed the diary of Caroline Seabury as a purposefully shaped work, patterned with dialogic functions.

5. Genealogical information on the Plimpton and Seabury families was compiled by Edith Seabury Nye, Shirley Pizziferri, Marjorie McMaster, and me from vital records of Chatham, Massachusetts; from U.S. census records; from genealogies of the Plimpton and Seabury families; and from newspaper clippings.

6. Caroline's diary entry for July 4, 1857, notes that during a seven-year period she lost her father, mother, brother, and five sisters to consumption and that now only she, one brother (Channing), and one sister (Martha) remained.

7. This information was gleaned from the Southbridge, Massachusetts, vital records by Shirley Pizziferri and Marjorie McMaster.

8. The 1850 federal census for Massachusetts shows Caroline Plimpton Seabury (aged 46) and her children Helen (aged 20), Martha (aged 11), and Channing (aged 8) living with Caroline's elder brother Stillman Plimpton and his second wife Mary Chamberlain Plimpton in Southbridge. Caroline Seabury the younger (aged 23) was apparently living on her own by this time.

9. According to Nancy Woloch, some of the earliest female institutes in the New England states included Emma Willard's Middlebury Female Seminary (founded in 1814) and her Troy Seminary (founded in 1821); Catharine Beecher's Hartford Female Seminary (founded in the 1820s); and Zilpah Grant's Ipswich Seminary (founded in 1828). Willard, Beecher, and Grant, along with other advocates of teacher training for women, argued

that women would make superior teachers to men because nature had designed women to care for children and to serve as moral guardians of youth. Teaching was considered a benevolent occupation for women, similar to missionary work (126–30).

Woloch has found that by 1850 in New England 75 percent of boys and girls attended school and that by 1850 half of the nation's women could read and write (125–26).

Nancy Hoffman notes that the Lexington Academy, in Lexington, Massachusetts, which opened in 1839, was the first normal school for women. Based on the model of the European *école normale*, its purpose was to form character for future teachers. Most students attended the Lexington Academy for one to two years prior to beginning their teaching (13–15).

In her study of the Troy Female Seminary, a model for many of the female seminaries that followed, Anne Firor Scott explains that the school's curriculum for women included mathematics, science, modern languages, Latin, history, philosophy, geography, and literature (9). Scott states that the 1870 federal census counted over two hundred thousand teachers in the nation's public elementary and secondary schools; more than half of these teachers were women (12).

Polly Welts Kaufman's in-depth study, *Women Teachers on the Frontier,* describes the training that several hundred young women received at a variety of female academies, seminaries, and institutes in the East prior to going West to work as teachers. Two primary motives cited for these young women's decisions to enter the teaching field were the economic necessity to be self-supporting and the sense of a mission to bring Protestant evangelical religion and education to the West (15–17).

10. According to Dr. W. L. Lipscomb's book, *A History of Columbus, Mississippi, During the 19th Century,* the Columbus Female Institute "was prosperous from the very start and well patronized by Columbus citizens and the adjoining counties. Most of the families in Columbus were represented, and the very elite and most literary of our Columbus women were pupils within its walls. Grandmothers and mothers remember it as the school in which they were educated and took their degrees, and while memory lasts the old people of Columbus will recall with gratitude and pleasure the Columbus Female Institute" (84).

Although the institute was destroyed by fire in the fall of 1858 while Caroline Seabury was teaching there, it was rebuilt and reopened in October 1860, then closed again during the Civil War and reopened in 1867. In 1884 it became the property of the state and the first state-supported school for women in the country. It was renamed the Mississippi Industrial Institute and College, functioning as a high school, vocational training institute, and college. Later its name was changed to the Mississippi State College for Women, and today it is known as the Mississippi University for Women.

11. An advertisement which appeared in *Keeler's Almanac* in 1854 described the Columbus Female Institute as being "upon a level with the best in the United States." The advertisement went on to say that

> Parents will find the Institute a safe and pleasant place to board their daughters. The Matron, Mrs. Curtiss, has for several years past, occupied a similar position in the Centenary Institute, and is peculiarly and eminently qualified for its important and responsible duties. The President and his family, and most of the Teachers, will reside in the Institute, and will cooperate with the Matron in the supervision and care of the Young Ladies.
>
> There will hereafter be but one Session per annum, commencing on the first Thursday of October, and closing on the Wednesday nearest the seventh of July. The faculty is as follows:
>
> Rev. B. F. Larrabee, President and Professor of Moral Philosophy.
> Thomas B. Bailey, Professor of Natural Science, and Teacher of Latin.
> J. W. M. Shattuck, Professor Mathematics.
> Mr. _____, Professor of Vocal and Instrumental Music.
> Mrs. M. A. Curtiss, Matron.
> Mrs. L. P. Larrabee, Teacher of Music.
> Mrs. E. E. Shattuck, Teacher of English.
> Miss C. R. Seabury, Teacher of French.
> Miss E. Hyde, Teacher of Music.
> Miss E. Abernathy, Teacher of Drawing, Painting, &c.
> Miss L. Street, Teacher of English.

For particular information, circulars, &c., apply at Columbus, Miss, to the President, or to the undersigned.

Stephen A. Brown
Secretary of the Board

12. At the time of her arrival in Columbus, Martha was sixteen. Caroline and Martha's eleven-year-old brother, Channing, remained in Brooklyn with the Plimpton family until his departure for St. Paul, Minnesota, in 1860.

13. According to information which I obtained from Samuel Kaye, the 1860 federal census lists Caroline Seabury as living in the boardinghouse of Benjamin S. Long in Columbus.

14. Waverly Plantation (also spelled Waverley) was developed by Colonel George Hampton Young, who first came to Mississippi from Petersburg, Georgia, during the 1830s to purchase the land which would become the plantation. Waverly is situated near the town of West Point, Mississippi, along the Tombigbee River. Before the mansion on the plantation was completed in 1852, Young's wife died, leaving him with ten children, some of whom were tutored by Caroline Seabury from 1862 to 1863.

Prior to the Civil War, Waverly became a well-known social center. During the war, it also served as a gathering place for Confederate leaders and their staffs. After the war ended in 1865, Colonel Young continued to live at Waverly until his death in 1880. His descendants lived in the mansion until 1913, when the last son died. After standing vacant for fifty years, the mansion was bought by Mr. and Mrs. Robert Allen Snow, who moved into it in 1962 and began restoration. Today Waverly is open year-round to the public. (This information was provided by Carolyn Neault and Samuel Kaye.)

15. The 1880 federal census data for Minnesota lists Carrie Seabury, aged 52, as living with Channing, Charles, and John Seabury at 195 East Eighth Street in St. Paul. The 1879–80 and 1880–81 St. Paul city directories list Miss Carrie Seabury as a boarder in the home of her brother Channing Seabury at 195 Eighth Street. After 1881, however, Caroline Seabury's name no longer appeared in St. Paul city directories, indicating that she did not continue to live with Channing after he remarried in 1883.

16. The 1895 federal census for Minnesota lists Channing and Elizabeth Seabury as living at 453 Ashland Avenue in St. Paul with their children John, Gerald, Paul, and Edith. Three women – Bridget and Elizabeth Maloney and Emma Benander – listed as "domestics," also composed the Seabury household. Oakland Cemetery records indicate that Channing and Elizabeth's son, Austin Summer Seabury, had died in 1889, shortly before his second birthday.

17. This information is carved on the large tombstone marking the Seabury family plot in Oakland Cemetery in St. Paul.

18. In a letter to me dated December 11, 1986, Edith Seabury Nye explained that she had never known her aunt Caroline (Edith was born in 1891, only two years before Caroline's death). Edith added that, when she and her mother emptied Caroline's trunk, which had remained in Channing and Elizabeth Seabury's attic for many years after Caroline's death, Edith's mother told her that Caroline had returned to the South during the final years of her life.

19. The certificate of death (no. 89301) states that Caroline Seabury, aged 65, who had been a resident of the District of Columbia for five months, died on March 18, 1893, of pneumonia brought on by pulmonary congestion. The death certificate also states that she was buried in St. Paul on March 20, 1893.

A brief death notice which appeared in the *St. Paul Dispatch* on March 20, 1893, states that Caroline Seabury's funeral would be held that day at her brother Channing's residence at 453 Ashland Avenue, St. Paul. Records for Oakland Cemetery in St. Paul list Caroline R. Seabury as buried in the Channing Seabury family plot (lot no. 14, block no. 18). Caroline's name is inscribed on the family tombstone just under her brother Channing's.

20. My interpretation of Caroline Seabury's diary as a family record has been influenced by Cynthia Huff's study of manuscript diaries by nine-

teenth-century British women, which analyzes the many ways in which diarists used their diaries to fashion family records. In her analysis of the diary of Louisa Galton, for instance, Huff discusses the ways in which the diarist created and symbolically altered the familial text by initially writing individual entries in either her voice or that of her husband and eventually symbolically silencing her husband by continuing to write entries in her voice alone ("From Faceless Chronicler" 99).

Similarly, Judy Lensink's work with the ten-volume diary of Emily Hawley Gillespie, a nineteenth-century American woman, reveals that the diarist began her diary in 1858 with the intention of making it into a record of her life. After her marriage and the births of her two children, Emily Gillespie continued to keep her diary as a family document, writing about each member's activities and often recopying old entries into newer journals to create a record of the Gillespie family's life (xii–xxvi).

Margo Culley explains that the modern idea of the diary as the "private arena of the 'secret self'" fails to take into account that the life recorded in many nineteenth-century diaries was "usually complexly woven with the life of family and community networks" ("Women's Diary Literature" 4). She also stresses that the diarist's perception of her intended audience "shapes the selection and arrangement of detail within the journal and determines more than anything else the kind of self-construction the diarist presents" (*Day at a Time* 12).

21. Fothergill defines this idea as follows: "As the diary grows to a certain length and substance it impresses upon the mind of its writer a conception of the completed book that might ultimately be, if sustained with sufficient dedication and vitality" (44). While Fothergill's work is based entirely on his study of published diaries by individuals who considered themselves writers, his concept of the "book of the self" is useful in studying unpublished diaries, such as Caroline Seabury's, which show evidence of the diarists' growing cognizance of their diaries as life stories.

22. As Fothergill puts it, "It is particularly common to find a diarist discovering in retrospect the book that he has been creating almost unwittingly; the diary so to speak becomes conscious of itself, and the writer grows to appreciate the shape that his own image and likeness have taken" (45).

23. In her study of relationships between black and white Southern women during the 1800s, Minrose Gwin discusses the opposite but mutually dependent roles into which these women were placed, and she assesses the resulting intensity of their feelings. For black and white women who wrote autobiographical accounts of their lives in the Old South, Gwin finds that the "the autobiographical mirror of self is therefore often dim and warped—by blindness, and by anger or denial engendered by that blindness" (12). Gwin discusses the often profound insights about racism inherent in such women's writings: "This critical intersection of race, gender, and re-

gion suggests too that issues of racism, perhaps of sexism as well, are so complexly interconnected to place that it is difficult and perhaps even impossible to examine them outside of a regional perspective. At the same time they are, even in their regionality, universal issues which touch us all" (6–16).

24. For a detailed discussion of these attributes, see Barbara Welter's landmark essay, "The Cult of True Womanhood: 1820–1860." Since the publication of Welter's essay in 1966, much attention has been focused on possible ways in which white middle- and upper-class American women managed to live within the confines of the Cult of True Womanhood while at the same time subverting it to meet their needs.

25. Steven E. Stowe explains that the female academy in the Old South had as its purpose the strengthening of family ties and the interlocking of generations through the perpetuation of cultural values—in short, bringing young girls into a "safe, social, and intellectually appropriate world which they would share while becoming women" (92). Yet the academy's role as parent and its students' role as sisters had its limits, as outlined by Stowe: "At the same time that academies created a sisterhood they ostensibly were training women to take their places in the heterosexual, risky world beyond the academy walls. From an educator's point of view, sisterhood among students might keep loneliness at bay in the short run and might stifle precocious thoughts of men, but it had little direct bearing on a grown woman's duties. After all, the true purpose of schooling was not to encourage a world of sisters" (94).

26. Margo Culley addresses this issue in describing the "special demands" made on the reader of diaries to participate actively in the process of re-creating the text: "As the journal pages construct continuity out of the apparent discontinuity created by time passing in the writer's life, the act of reading may generate a parallel process for the reader" (*Day at a Time* 24).

27. I have discussed this issue in greater detail in articles in *Studies in Autobiography* (1988), *A/B: Auto/biography Studies* (1986), *Women's Studies International Forum* (1987), *Women's Studies Quarterly* (1989), and *Legacy* (forthcoming).

In addition, several recent books on women's autobiography raise similar questions. For instance, the editors of *Interpreting Women's Lives* analyze context as a dynamic, interactive process which "requires us to choose among the multiple identities and associations shaping a life" and which "involves understanding the meaning of a life in its narrator's frame of reference, and making sense of that life from the different and necessarily comparative frame of reference of the interpreter" (Personal Narratives Group 19).

At the heart of the matter is the issue of reflexivity, that is, the reader/interpreter's willingness to examine the assumptions and biases that influence his or her research. Central to the concept of reflexivity, according to

Barbara Myerhoff and Jay Ruby, is the researcher's "deliberate, intentional revelation" to an audience of the factors that have caused him or her to ask questions, seek answers, and present findings in certain ways (6).

In my work with issues of reflexivity, I have found Clifford Geertz's observation most helpful: "Finding somewhere to stand in a text that is supposed to be at one and the same time an intimate view and a cool assessment is almost as much of a challenge as gaining the view and making the assessment in the first place" (10).

The Diary of Caroline Seabury

1. Caroline's traveling companions included Abram Murdock, a prominent merchant and owner of Hale and Murdock, a wholesale and retail trading business in Columbus, Mississippi. He was a trustee of the Columbus Female Institute. Mr. Murdock's nephew and another teacher, Miss Smith, also accompanied Caroline on her journey.

2. At that time no direct rail line ran from Washington, D.C., to Richmond or Petersburg, Virginia. Caroline and her companions had to take a steamer down the Potomac River to Aquia (also spelled Acquia) Creek and from there a train for Richmond.

3. "First Families of Virginia," members of which claimed to be able to trace their ancestry back to the Mayflower voyagers.

4. Although Caroline's immediate ancestors were from the Cape Cod area of Chatham and Eastham, some of her Seabury ancestors may also have lived in Camden, South Carolina.

5. The Mr. and Mrs. Smith referred to here are other passengers; they are not the parents of the Miss Smith who accompanied Caroline to Columbus.

6. The title character of British writer William Cowper's poem, "The Diverting History of John Gilpin," published in 1785. John Gilpin, a linen-draper, and his wife decided to celebrate their twentieth anniversary by taking a trip from Ware to Edmonton. Cowper's poem describes the Gilpin family's unpredictable and often hazardous journey.

7. Disastrous fires had just swept through Columbus, destroying more than half of the business district. Following the fires, the Board of Aldermen passed an ordinance requiring all city buildings to be fireproofed (*City of Columbus Early Minute Book*).

8. Caroline and her companions went directly to the Columbus Female Institute, which stood on the site of what is now the Mississippi University for Women.

9. The Reverend R. A. Means, along with his wife and two daughters, lived at the Columbus Female Institute. Rev. Means served as presi-

dent for several years and was succeeded by Mr. J. H. McLean and then by Rev. B. F. Larrabee.

10. Later in her diary, on July 4, 1857, Caroline wrote that she had lost both parents, one brother, and five sisters to consumption, today known as tuberculosis. Consumption, a highly communicable disease, affected the lungs, leading to hemorrhaging, debilitation, and eventual death.

11. The opening line of Percy Bysshe Shelley's "To a Sky-Lark" (1820).

12. The plantation to which Caroline's friend Mr. C. took her was probably Waverly, near West Point, Mississippi, where Caroline would later tutor the daughters of Colonel George Hampton Young, the owner.

13. Mr. J. Hamilton was the son of Alexander Hamilton. Caroline may have become friends with J. Hamilton through his brother, Alexander Hamilton, Jr., who was married to Anna Young, one of the daughters of Colonel George Hampton Young. As Caroline's diary entry unfolds, the reader learns that Anne was fathered by her master, Judge Nash. Thus Anne was a half-sister of her mistress, Miss Maria Nash.

14. From Shakespeare's *Titus Andronicus*, act 4, scene 1, lines 34–35.

15. From Shakespeare's *A Midsummer Night's Dream,* act 3, scene 2, lines 198–99.

16. The *City of Columbus Early Minute Book* notes that on April 23, 1857, a case of smallpox was reported on Square 30, north of Main Street. The victim, John Dupree, was quarantined at the home of his mother. The entry for April 27, 1857, states that all physicians must notify the Committee of Health of all contagious diseases and that a suitable building would be provided as a hospital.

17. The *City of Columbus Early Minute Book* entry for May 6, 1857, states that a "suitable testimonial" would be presented to "Miss Caroline A. Seabrey" on behalf of the board in appreciation for her "voluntary efforts to relieve those suffering under the small-pox lately visited our city." A newspaper clipping entitled "Nobly Done," pasted into Caroline's diary, quotes the board's commendation and provides Caroline's reply.

18. Caroline's parents, John and Caroline Seabury; her half-sisters Julia, Lucretia, and Maria; her brother John; and her sisters Mary and Helen.

19. Francis Bacon (1561–1626), British essayist and magistrate, advocated the development of a scientific method with emphasis on verifiable experimentation. In *The Advancement of Learning,* published in 1605, Bacon argued in favor of scientific hypothesis and verification, with emphasis on accuracy of language.

20. The Friendship Cemetery in Columbus, Mississippi, has been in existence since the 1840s. It contains the graves of about sixteen hundred Confederate soldiers as well as several Confederate generals and Mississippi governors. Friendship Cemetery is listed on the National Register of Historic Places. A map of the cemetery shows that Martha Seabury's grave in

lot no. 13 North is near the side of the cemetery that borders on Fourth Street South in Columbus (personal correspondence from Samuel Kaye, November 3, 1987).

21. The *Wanderer,* owned by Charles A. L. Lamar, a member of a wealthy Southern family, was the most well known of the slave trade schooners which illegally transported Africans to the Uinted States during the mid- 1800s. In 1858 the ship, carrying five hundred Africans and bound for Georgia, was stopped by the government and ordered back to Africa. Lamar, along with his crew, was arrested but later acquitted by jurors in Savannah. The four hundred Africans who survived the voyage to Georgia were then smuggled into the South and sold, as Caroline noted in this diary entry (McPherson 103).

22. Caroline's aunt and uncle, Maria and Edwin Plimpton, had a summer home in Manchester, Vermont, not far from the New York state line. Caroline spent the summer of 1859 in Manchester with her brother Channing and her aunt and uncle's family.

23. The Democratic National Convention, held at Institute Hall in Charleston, South Carolina, got under way in April 1860. Heated and bitter debates ensued over the party's platform stance and language on slavery. After the majority of convention delegates had voted to accept a party platform not to the liking of the Southern states, seven Southern states with fifty delegates withdrew their support, and the party was split. As the convention continued and balloting on the party's presidential nominee dragged on, the Southerners who had seceded from the convention held an organizational meeting in Military Hall in Charleston and formed their own convention, passing a strongly proslavery platform.

The Democratic National Convention adjourned, then reconvened in Baltimore on June 18, 1860. When it appeared certain that Stephen A. Douglas would be the party's presidential nominee, the delegates from Virginia withdrew from the convention, followed by several delegates from North Carolina, Maryland, and Tennessee. Once again a second convention was organized by these forces and other dissatisfied Democratic delegates. It quickly passed a proslavery platform to counter the official platform.

Bruce Catton summarizes the events of that spring and summer as follows: "At Charleston and at Baltimore the South had taken its stand. It would remain the South, separate and unalterable. He who could not subscribe to that fact would be an enemy" (78).

24. Caroline's cautious *Nous verrons* (We shall see) echoed the sentiments of countless Americans. On November 6, 1860, Abraham Lincoln was elected president of the United States. Lincoln received 54 percent of the Northern popular vote, 40 percent of the national popular vote, and 180 electoral votes (McPherson 232).

Lincoln was at the Illinois statehouse in Springfield when he received word of his election. Bruce Catton describes the reaction across the country: "Charleston was as jubilant and as excited as Springfield, and there were as many flags and black-powder salutes along the Battery as in front of the Illinois state house. Here too there was a feeling of release from tension. Whatever the future might conceal, one pressure at least had been discharged. This Republican triumph, by its very completeness, was so intolerable that men would behave in a new way. There would be a new nation, it would be born in South Carolina, and it would begin to take shape at once" (111–12).

25. South Carolina seceded from the Union on December 20, 1860. Mississippi seceded on January 9, 1861, followed by Florida, Alabama, Georgia, Louisiana, and Texas. The second wave of secession, following the victory of Southern forces at Fort Sumter in April 1861, included Virginia, Arkansas, North Carolina, and Tennessee. In all, eleven Southern states seceded to form the Confederate States of America.

26. Fort Pickens, located on an island at the mouth of Pensacola Bay, and Fort Sumter, on an island in Charlestown harbor, were the only two pieces of Southern property left in Union hands in early 1861. After the surrender of Fort Sumter of April 14, 1861, Fort Pickens also passed into Confederate hands (McPherson 263ff).

27. Only about four thousand rounds of ammunition were fired during the siege of Fort Sumter, which lasted from April 12 to 14, 1861. After the Confederate flag had been raised over the fort, General P. G. T. Beauregard and other officials inspected the damages, estimating that the necessary repairs would cost approximately $350,000 (Catton 326).

28. Big Bethel, located north of Newport News, Virginia, was the site of a battle between Union forces, commanded by Major General Benjamin F. Butler, and Confederate forces, commanded by General J. B. Magruder. Union troops became confused and fired into their own ranks, leading to seventy-six Union casualties and victory for the Confederates (Foote 56).

29. The first battle of Manassas / Bull Run, Virginia, occurred on July 21, 1861, and was one of the first major victories for the Confederate forces. It also shook the confidence of Union forces that the war would be easily won. Generals P. G. T. Beauregard and Joseph Johnston led Southern forces in a rout of Union troops. Union casualties stood at approximately three thousand while Confederate casualties totaled approximately two thousand (Foote 84). During this battle Confederate general Barnard Bee saw General Thomas J. Jackson's Virginia troops holding the line on Henry House Hill. General Bee pointed to Jackson's troops and said something like, "Look, there is Jackson standing like a stone wall! Rally behind the Virginians!" Thenceforth, General Jackson became known as Stonewall and his troops as the Stonewall Brigade (McPherson 342).

30. The battle for Fort Donelson followed on the heels of the Union victory at Fort Henry, Tennessee, which was surrendered by Confederate forces on Feburary 6, 1862. Fort Donelson, a stockade that enclosed soldiers' dwellings and equipment, guarded the riverine approach to Nashville. General Ulysses S. Grant sent fifteen thousand Union troops there on February 12, 1862. Ten thousand Union reinforcements arrived on February 14, and on February 16 the Confederate forces surrendered. The surrender of Fort Donelson signaled the Union forces' rapid advance toward taking control of all of Kentucky and most of Tennessee by the spring of 1862 (McPherson 396–403).

31. On February 22, 1862, Jefferson Davis was inaugurated in Richmond for a six-year term as president of the Confederate States. Davis had served as provisional president until a general election in November 1861, when he and Alexander H. Stephens were elected president and vice-president without opposition. In his inaugural address, Davis urged his fellow Southerners to renew their commitment to their cause despite recent reversals (McPherson 403).

32. The battle of Shiloh, or Pittsburgh Landing, which took place in early April 1862, was the first major bloodbath of the Civil War. Confederate troops appeared to have routed Yankee forces on April 6, but on the following day General Ulysses S. Grant's troops staged a counterattack and sent the Southern forces into retreat. Of the approximately one hundred thousand soldiers who fought on both sides, one out of four was killed, wounded, or captured (Foote 350). As James McPherson notes, "Gone was the romantic innocence of Rebs and Yanks who had marched off to war in 1861" (413).

33. Confederate generals Albert Sidney Johnston and P. G. T. Beauregard led the Southern troops into battle at Shiloh. Johnston was killed during the battle.

34. Following General Ulysses S. Grant's counterattack on Beauregard and Johnston's troops, the Confederate forces retreated, and hordes of wounded and sick soldiers were sent to Columbus to be cared for by the townspeople.

35. By late April 1862 the Union forces had captured Memphis and turned it into a base for further operations on the Mississippi. The Union naval forces, led by Flag Officer David Farragut, attacked the river batteries below New Orleans on the morning of April 25. On April 29 Farragut raised the Union flag over the city (McPherson 418–20).

36. Major General Benjamin F. Butler, who led the Union forces in occupying New Orleans, quickly earned a reputation as a harsh and punitive man. Once he hanged a man for wearing a remnant of Union bunting torn from a public building, and another time he issued an order dictating that any woman caught showing contempt for Union forces would be treated

as "a woman of the town plying her avocation" (Foote 533–34). Southerners were incensed by the tactics of Beast Butler, as Caroline noted in this entry.

37. The Reverend B. F. Larrabee was the principal who relieved Caroline of her teaching duties at the Columbus Female Institute, whereupon Caroline found work tutoring the daughters of Colonel George Hampton Young at Waverly. It was not uncommon for Northerners employed in the South to lose their positions just prior to and during the Civil War. As James McPherson explains, "Every Yankee in the South became *persona non grata.* Some of them received a coat of tar and feathers and a ride out of town on a rail. A few were lynched. The citizens of Boggy Swamp, South Carolina, ran two northern tutors out of the district. . . . The northern-born president of an Alabama college had to flee for his life" (213). Such information makes more understandable Caroline's perception that she needed to keep silent as a Northern woman in Mississippi.

38. The preacher is referring to Zacchaeus the publican, mentioned in the Gospel of Luke, chapter 19. Because Zacchaeus, who wanted to see Jesus, was "small of stature," he climbed into a sycamore tree for a better view. Jesus saw Zacchaeus, called him down, and went to stay at his house, telling him that he had been saved that day.

39. On September 22, 1862, Abraham Lincoln told his cabinet of his plan to issue the Emancipation Proclamation if the Union army drove the Confederates out of Maryland. Lincoln planned that the proclamation would take effect on January 1, 1863. It stated that all slaves living in states in rebellion against the United States government on that date would be freed. It did not address the status of slaves in areas not in rebellion against the U.S. government. As president, Lincoln had no constitutional power to take action against slavery in loyal areas (McPherson 557–58). For this and other reasons, some labeled the Emancipation Proclamation a meaningless gesture on Lincoln's part.

40. During April 1863 Union forces were conducting expeditions across Mississippi en route to Vicksburg. The Yankee troops who passed through Columbus were no doubt part of these expeditionary forces.

41. Lieut. Hamilton is Confederate lieutenant Alexander Hamilton, the husband of Anna Young, daughter of George Hampton Young. His return to Waverly would have been considered essential because it was thought unseemly and dangerous to leave white women in charge of slaves on plantations. In September 1862 the Confederate Congress had passed a statute exempting from military service one white man on every plantation that had twenty or more slaves. The "Twenty Negro" law was highly unpopular in the South because it extended exemption from military duty to Southern planters, already a privileged class (McPherson 611–12).

42. The siege of Vicksburg lasted from May until July 1863, with the

key battle taking place at Champion's Hill on May 16, 1863. Confederate general John Pemberton unconditionally surrendered his forces to General Ulysses S. Grant on July 4, 1863. The capture of Vicksburg was, according to James McPherson, the "most important northern strategic victory of the war" (637).

43. The injunction "as long as you ken live together" stands in sharp contrast to "as long as you both shall live." Marriages between slaves held no guarantees, as sales could break up families and separate husbands and wives. About one-fourth of slave marriages were broken by owners or heirs who sold or moved husbands and wives apart (McPherson 38).

44. Confederate brigadier general James R. Chalmers gave chase to Union forces scattered throughout the area near Columbus.

45. A sarcastic reference to members of the "First Families" of Mississippi.

46. "Manifest Destiny" referred to the widely held belief that the United States was destined to continue its expansion into foreign territories with the goal of bringing them into the Union. During the Civil War the concept of manifest destiny took on specific dimensions as pro- and antislavery factions argued whether slavery ought to continue to exist only in states where it already did exist or whether it should be permitted in states newly entering the Union. According to Peter Parish, "That very Manifest Destiny which had been partly inspired by a sense of national mission was to create bitter sectional contention, as pro-slavery expansionists looked for fresh fields to conquer, and anti-slavery men sought to pen slavery within its existing limits" (31).

47. Meg Merrills refers to Meg Merrilies, the wild old gypsy in Sir Walter Scott's novel *Guy Mannering.*

48. After Union forces had occupied areas of the South, they began offering Southerners the opportunity to take loyalty oaths, pledging fidelity to the United States government in return for kind treatment. In December 1863 Lincoln proposed the idea of a formal loyalty oath in his message to Congress. If a Southerner took an oath of future loyalty to the United States, then that individual would be pardoned and his property rights would be restored. Lincoln's plan met with a good deal of skepticism among those who argued that the simple taking of an oath could not guarantee faithfulness to the Union. Some Southerners loyal to the Confederate cause nonetheless took the loyalty oath as a precaution against punishment by Yankee troops (Parish 523–24).

49. By the end of August 1863 Union troops had occupied most of the area through which Caroline and her companions traveled on their way to the Mississippi River. Yankee raids on plantations and farms, such as the one described in this diary passage, were common ways for Northern troops to seize supplies, leaving many Southerners destitute.

50. The guarantee of protection from prosecution offered to any individual who would sign an oath of loyalty to the United States government.

51. *Brogans* are coarse, ankle-high work shoes.

52. *Godey's Ladies Book,* edited by Sarah Josepha Hale, was the premier women's magazine of its day. Hale published articles centering on "women's sphere" activities—with titles such as "Maternal Counsels to a Daughter," "How to Make Wax Flowers and Fruit," and "Model Cottages." By 1860 *Godey's* had over 160,000 subscribers (Woloch 98ff).

53. *Copperhead* was a pejorative term used to refer to a member of the antiwar faction of the Democratic party. The strongest opposition to the war was in the northwestern states of Illinois, Indiana, and Ohio. Feeling against copperheads ran high in the Northern states throughout the Civil War.

54. John Hunt Morgan's Confederate cavalry division staged many raids behind Union lines in Kentucky. In July 1863 Morgan took his troops across the Ohio River into Indiana and Ohio, where he was captured by Union forces and imprisoned in the state penitentiary, from which he escaped in November 1863 (McPherson 763).

Bibliography

❦

Alexander, Ilene, Suzanne Bunkers, and Cherry Muhanji. "A Conversation on Studying and Writing about Women's Lives Using Nontraditional Methodologies." *Women's Studies Quarterly* 17.3–4 (Fall/Winter 1989): 99–114.

Beauchamp, Virginia, ed. *A Private War: Letters and Diaries of Madge Preston, 1862–1867.* New Brunswick: Rutgers U P, 1987.

Billington, Ray Allen, ed. *The Journal of Charlotte L. Forten: A Free Negro in the Slave Era.* New York: Norton, 1953.

Bloom, Lynn Z. "Collaboration and Control: Editors and Autobiographies." Modern Language Association Convention. December 1988.

Bloom, Lynn Z., ed. *Forbidden Family: A Wartime Memoir of the Philippines, 1941–1945.* By Margaret Sams. Madison: U of Wisconsin P, 1989.

Brumgardt, John R., ed. *Civil War Nurse: The Diary and Letters of Hannah Ropes.* Knoxville: U of Tennessee P, 1980.

Bunkers, Suzanne L. "Diaries: Public *and* Private Records of Women's Lives." *Legacy: A Journal of Nineteenth-Century American Women Writers.* Forthcoming.

Bunkers, Suzanne L. "'Faithful Friend': Nineteenth-Century Midwestern American Women's Unpublished Diaries." *Women's Studies International Forum* 10.1 (1987): 7–17.

Bunkers, Suzanne L. "Midwestern Diaries and Journals: What Women Were (Not) Saying in the Late 1800s." *Studies in Autobiography.* Ed. James Olney. New York: Oxford U P, 1988. 190–210.

Bunkers, Suzanne L. "Reading and Interpreting Unpublished Diaries by Nineteenth-Century Women." *A/B: Auto/biography Studies* 2.2 (Summer 1986): 15–17.

Catton, Bruce. *The Coming Fury.* Vol. 1 of *The Centennial History of the Civil War.* New York: Simon, 1967.

City of Columbus Early Minute Book. Columbus, MS. Unpublished record book.

Cott, Nancy. *The Bonds of Womanhood: "Woman's Sphere" in New England, 1780–1835.* New Haven: Yale U P, 1977.

Culley, Margo, ed. *A Day at a Time: The Diary Literature of American Women from 1764 to the Present.* New York: Feminist, 1985.

Bibliography

Culley, Margo. "Women's Diary Literature: Resources and Directions in the Field." *Legacy* 1.1 (Spring 1984): 4–5.

Foote, Shelby. *The Civil War: A Narrative*. Vols. 1 and 2. New York: Random, 1958.

Fothergill, Robert. *Private Chronicles: A Study of English Diaries*. New York: Oxford U P, 1974.

Fox-Genovese, Elizabeth. *Within the Plantation Household: Black and White Women of the Old South*. Chapel Hill: U of North Carolina P, 1988.

Geertz, Clifford. *Words and Lives: The Anthropologist as Author*. Stanford: Stanford U P, 1988.

Gwin, Minrose C. *Black and White Women of the Old South: The Peculiar Sisterhood in American Literature*. Knoxville: U of Tennessee P, 1985.

Hampsten, Elizabeth. *Read This Only to Yourself: The Private Writings of Midwestern Women, 1880–1910*. Bloomington: Indiana U P, 1982.

Hoffman, Nancy. *Woman's "True" Profession: Voices from the History of Teaching*. Old Westbury, NY: Feminist, 1981.

Hogan, Rebecca S. "Diarists on Diaries." *A/B: Auto/biography Studies* 2.2 (Summer 1986): 9–14.

Hogan, Rebecca S. "Engendered Autobiography: The Diary as a Feminine Form." *Prose Studies*. Forthcoming.

Huff, Cynthia. *British Women's Diaries: A Descriptive Bibliography of Selected Nineteenth-Century Women's Manuscript Diaries*. New York: AMS, 1985.

Huff, Cynthia. "From Faceless Chronicler to Self-Creator: The Diary of Louisa Galton, 1830–1896. *Biography* 10.2 (Spring 1987): 95–106.

Huff, Cynthia. "Text as Process: Learning How to Read the Unpublished Diary." Modern Language Association Convention. December 1987.

Kaufman, Polly Welts. *Women Teachers on the Frontier*. New Haven: Yale U P, 1984.

Lensink, Judy Nolte, ed. *"A Secret to Be Burried": The Diary and Life of Emily Hawley Gillespie, 1858–1888*. Iowa City: U of Iowa P, 1989.

Lipscomb, W. L. *A History of Columbus, Mississippi, During the 19th Century*. Columbus, MS, 1909.

McPherson, James M. *Battle Cry of Freedom: The Civil War Era*. New York: Oxford U P, 1988.

Marcus, Jane. "Invisible Mending." *Between Women: Biographers, Novelists, Critics, Teachers, and Artists Write about Their Work on Women*. Ed. Carol Ascher, Louise DeSalvo, and Sara Ruddick. Boston: Beacon, 1984. 381–95.

Melder, Keith E. "Woman's High Calling: The Teaching Profession in America, 1830–1860." *American Studies* 13.2 (Fall 1972): 19–32.

Myerhoff, Barbara, and Jay Ruby. *A Crack in the Mirror: Reflexivity and Its Relatives*. Philadelphia: U of Pennsylvania P, 1982.

Parish, Peter J. *The American Civil War.* New York: Holmes & Meier, 1975.

Personal Narratives Group, ed. *Interpreting Women's Lives: Feminist Theory and Personal Narratives.* Bloomington: Indiana U P, 1989.

Schwartz, Gerald, ed. *A Woman Doctor's Civil War: Esther Hill Hawks' Diary.* Columbia: U of South Carolina P, 1984.

Scott, Ann Firor. "The Ever Widening Circle: The Diffusion of Feminist Values from the Troy Female Seminary, 1822–1872." *History of Education Quarterly* 19 (Spring 1979): 3–26.

Seabury, Channing, and Family Papers. Minnesota Historical Society, St. Paul, MN.

Showalter, Elaine. "Piecing and Writing." *The Poetics of Gender.* Ed. Nancy K. Miller. New York: Columbia U P, 1986. 222–47.

Stowe, Steven E. "The Not-So-Cloistered Academy: Elite Women's Education and Family Feeling in the Old South." *The Web of Southern Social Relations: Women, Family, & Education.* Ed. Walter J. Fraser, Jr., R. Frank Saunders, Jr., and Jon L. Wakelyn. Athens: U of Georgia P, 1985. 90–106.

Thomas, Trudelle H. "Convent Daybooks and Deathbooks: Writing the Communal Myth." Modern Language Association Convention. December 1987.

Thomas, Trudelle H. "Women's Diaries of the Westward Movement: A Methodological Study." *Forum: A Women's Studies Quarterly* 10.3 (Spring 1984): 7, 9–11.

Welter, Barbara. "The Cult of True Womanhood: 1820–1860." *American Quarterly* 18 (Summer 1966): 151–74.

Woloch, Nancy. *Women and the American Experience.* New York: Knopf, 1984.

Woods, K. G., Shiela C. Robertson, and Kathleen Ann O'Brien. *A Social History of Women: Caroline Seabury.* St. Louis Park, MN: Upper Midwest Women's History Center for Teachers, 1982.

Woodward, C. Vann, and Elisabeth Muhlenfeld, eds. *The Private Mary Chesnut: The Unpublished Civil War Diaries.* New York: Oxford U P, 1984.

Index

A/B: Auto/biography Studies, 129*n27*
Aberdeen, Miss., 56
Abolitionists, 32
Acquia Creek. *See* Aquia Creek
Advancement of Learning, The, 131*n19*.
   See also Bacon, Sir Francis
Africans: as slaves, 55, 132*n21*
Alabama, 49; secession, 133*n25*
Albany, N.Y., 115
Allen, Brother (preacher), 71
Amelia (cook at Waverly), 76
Anne (half-sister of Maria Nash), 44–
   45, 131*n13*
Aquia Creek, 28, 62, 130*n2*
Arkansas: secession of, 133*n25*
Augusta, Ga., 31, 32

Bacon, Sir Francis, 51, 131*n19*
Baltimore, Md., 25, 61, 132*n23*
Barker, Antonia (cousin of Caroline),
   115
Barker, Messr. (cousin of Caroline), 114
Beauregard, Pierre Gustave Toutant
   (Confederate general), 60, 65,
   133*n29*, 134*n33*
Bee, Bernard (Confederate general),
   133*n29*
Beecher, Catherine (founder of Hart-
   ford Female Seminary), 124–25*n9*
Benander, Emma (domestic servant in
   Seabury household), 127*n16*
Big Bethel, battle of, 63, 133*n28*
Black women in the Old South: their
   relationships with white women,
   18, 128–29*n23*. *See also* Gwin,
   Minrose
"The Blue and the Gray" (poem in
   The Atlantic Monthly), 117

Boston, Mass., 115
Broadway, New York City, 115
Brogans, 104, 137*n51*
Brooklyn, N.Y., 3, 7, 8, 11, 16, 25,
   114, 115, 126*n12*
Brown, George C., 54
Buck Island (on Mississippi River),
   105, 108
Bull Run, first battle of, 63, 133*n29*.
   See also Manassas Gap
Bunkers, Suzanne, 129*n27*
Bush, Amanda, 69
Butler, Benjamin Franklin (Confeder-
   ate general), 69, 133*n29*, 134*n33*,
   134–35*n36*

Cairo, Ill., 113
Calhoun County, Miss., 91
Camden, S.C., 130*n4*
Cape Cod, Mass.: Caroline's blood,
   32; Caroline as native of, 45; Chat-
   ham and Eastham, 130*n4*. *See also*
   Chatham, Mass.; Eastham, Mass.
Cape Fear River, 30
Carroll Park, No. 3 (home of Edwin
   and Maria Plimpton), 116
Carson, Miss., 95
Catton, Bruce, 132*n23*, 132–33*n24*,
   133*n27*
Chalmers, James Ronald (Confederate
   general), 84, 96, 106, 107, 136*n44*
Champion's Hill, Miss., battle of,
   135–36*n42*. *See also* Vicksburg
Charles: wedding of, 18, 78
Charleston, S.C.: 1860 Convention of,
   59, 60, 132*n23*
Charlestown Harbor, 133*n26*
Charon and the Styx, 31

Chatham, Mass., 124*n5*, 130*n4*
Chesnut, Mary: diary of, 19
Chickasaw County, Miss., 89, 94
Cincinnati, Oh., 11, 111, 113, 114, 115
City of Columbus Early Minute Book,
    130*n7*, 131*nn16–17*
Civil War, 10, 14, 15, 19, 20, 60–116
    passim, 133*nn26–29*, 134*nn30–35*,
    134–35*n36*, 135*nn39–41*, 135–36*n42*,
    136*nn44,46,48–49*, 137*nn50,53–54*
Clayton, George R., 51
Clayton, Squire, 91
Cleveland, Oh., 115
Coffee-ville, Miss., 92
Colin, Uncle (carriage driver), 75
Columbus, Oh., 115
Columbus, Miss., 3, 7, 8, 10, 16, 25,
    35, 47, 50, 65, 108, 120, 125*n10*,
    126*nn12–13*, 130*n1*, 131*nn16–17,20*,
    135*n37*
Columbus Female Institute, 3, 7, 8,
    10, 18, 35, 125*n10*, 126*n11*, 130*n8*,
    135*n37*
Confederate Army, 11, 60, 63, 65, 70,
    76, 87, 90, 99, 131–32*n20*,
    133*nn26–27,29*, 134*nn30,32–35*,
    134–35*n36*, 135*nn39–40*, 135–
    36*n42*, 136*nn44,48–49*, 137*n54*
Confederate Congress, 103, 135*n41*
Confederate States of America, 65, 96,
    100, 103, 133*n25*, 134*n31*
Consumption, 3, 6, 10, 50, 52,
    124*n6*, 131*n10*
"Copperhead," 113, 137*n53*
Country barbeque and wedding,
    Caroline's account of, 77–79
Cruft, Frances Warren (first wife of
    Channing Seabury), 11, 13
Crusoe, Robinson, 106
Culley, Margo, 124*n4*, 127–28*n20*,
    129*n26*
Cult of True Womanhood, 129*n24*. *See
    also* Proper Sphere; Welter, Barbara

Dale, E. W., 77
Dan (assistant in Caroline's escape), 11,
    82–105 *passim*

Davis, Jefferson (President of the Con-
    federate States of America), 20, 65,
    118, 119, 134*n31*
Day at a Time, 124*n4*, 127–28*n20*,
    129*n26*. *See also* Culley, Margo
Denison, Camp, 115
Diary: as form of autobiography, 14–
    15; as serial autobiography, 16–17;
    as "book of the self," 128*n21*; dona-
    tion of Caroline's to MHS, 4; Caro-
    line's as historical document, 11; as
    collaborative text, 16; and context,
    129*n27*; defined, 123*n1*; as dialogic
    work, 124*n4*; as familial or com-
    munal text, 127–28*n20*; as shaped
    text, 19; as verbal construct, 124*n4*
Donelson, Fort, battle of, 64, 134*n30*
Donnell, Levi, 51, 54
Douglas, Stephen A., 132*n23*
Dupree, John, 9, 131*n16*
Dupree, Mrs. (mother of John Du-
    pree), 47

Eastham, Mass., 130*n4*
école normale, 125*n9*
Editor, role of, 17, 19–21
Emancipation Proclamation, 74, 86,
    135*n39*
Eve, Dr., 66

Farragut, David (Union flag officer),
    134*n35*
Female Academy: history of, 7; female
    teacher's role in, 18–19; role in per-
    petuating cultural values, 129*n25*
Female Institute. *See* Female Academy
Female Seminary. *See* Female Academy
FFVs (First Families of Virginia), 29,
    130*n3*
Finsey, Messr., 114
First Families of Mississippi, 86, 136*n45*
Fiske, Kezia (grandmother of Caroline
    Seabury), 6
Fiske, Lydia (sister of Kezia Fiske), 6
Florida: secession of, 133*n25*
Foote, Shelby, 133*nn28–29*, 134*n32*,
    134–35*n36*

Forten, Charlotte L.: journal of, 19
Fothergill, Robert, 16, 128*nn21–22*
Friendship Cemetery, 10, 54, 131–
32*n20*

Gayoso House Hotel, 111
Geertz, Clifford, 129–30*n27*
Georgia: secession of, 133*n25*
Gerdine, General, 81
Gerdine, Mrs., 81
Gettysburg, Pa., battle of, 81
Gillespie, Emily Hawley: diary of, 19
Gilpin, John, 34, 130*n6*
Godey's Ladies Book, 112, 137*n52*
Governor's Island, N.Y., 25
Grant, Ulysses Simpson (Union gen-
eral), 65, 76, 134*n32*, 135–36*n42*
Grant, Zilpah (founder of Ipswich
Seminary), 124–25*n9*
Great Pedee River, 30
Greenwood, Miss., 93
Guy Mannering, 136*n47*. *See also* Scott,
Sir Walter
Gwin, Minrose, 128–29*n23*. *See also*
Black women in the Old South

Hale, Harrison, 54
Hale, Sarah Josepha (editor of *Godey's
Ladies Book*), 137*n52*
Hamburg, 32
Hamilton, Alexander, Jr. (Confederate
lieutenant), 76, 131*n13*, 134*n41*
Hamilton, Alexander, Sr., 131*n13*
"Hard Shell Baptist Sermon," Caro-
line's account of, 71–73
Harper's Illustrated, 112
Harris, (Confederate general), 75
Hartford Female Seminary, 124–25*n9*.
See also Catherine Beecher
Hawks, Esther Hill: diary of, 19
Henry, Fort, battle of, 134*n30*
*History of Columbus, Mississippi, During
the 19th Century, A*, 125*n10*. *See also*
Lipscomb, W. L.
Hoffman, Nancy, 123*n2*, 124–25*n9*
Hogan, Rebecca, 124*n4*

Hudson, Fort, 81, 87
Huff, Cynthia, 127–28*n20*

Illinois, 137*n53*
Indiana, 137*nn53,54*
Interpreting Women's Lives, 129–30*n27*.
See also Personal Narratives Group
Ipswich Seminary, 124–25*n9*. *See also*
Grant, Zilpah

Jack (assistant in Caroline's escape), 11,
82–105 *passim*
Jack (Suey's husband), 41–42
Jackson, Thomas J. ("Stonewall")
(Confederate general), 133*n29*
Jersey City Ferry, 25
Joe (slave sold at auction), 42
John (Anne's husband), 44
Johnston, Albert Sidney (Confederate
general), 65, 134*n33*
Johnston, Joseph (Confederate gen-
eral), 133*n29*

Kaufman, Polly Welts, 124–25*n9*. *See
also Women Teachers on the Frontier*
Kaye, Samuel, 126–27*n14*, 131–
32*n20*
Keeler's Almanac: advertisement for
Columbus Female Institute, 126*n11*
Kentucky, 134*n30*, 137*n54*

Lamar, Charles A. L., 132*n21*
Larabee, B. F., 125*n11*, 130–31*n9*,
135*n37*
Lensink, Judy, 124*n4*, 127–28*n20*
Lexington Academy, 124–25*n9*
Lincoln, Abraham (President of the
United States), 59, 60, 61, 74, 86,
119, 132–33*n24*, 135*n39*, 136*n48*
Lipscomb, W. L. (author of history of
Columbus, Mississippi), 125*n10*
Long, Mrs., 68
Louisiana: secession of, 133*n25*
Lowell, Charles Russell, Jr. (Confeder-
ate general), 68
Lowndes County, Miss., 80, 120

Loyalty Oath, 106, 136*n48*, 137*n50*.
  See also Protection Papers
Lyon, Dr., 111

McLean, J. H., 130–31*n9*
McMaster, Marjorie, 124*nn5,7*
McPherson, James, 132*nn21,24*,
  133*nn26,29*, 134*nn30–32,35*,
  135*nn37,39,41*, 136*nn42–43*,
  137*n54*
Magruder, J. B. (Confederate general),
  133*n28*
Maloney, Bridget (domestic servant in
  Seabury household), 127*n16*
Maloney, Elizabeth (domestic servant
  in Seabury household), 127*n16*
Manassas Gap (Bull Run), first battle
  of, 63, 133*n29*
Manchester, Vt., 10, 56, 132*n22*
Manifest Destiny, 86, 136*n46*
Maria: wedding of, 18, 78
Maryland: secession of, 132*n23*, 135*n39*
Massachusetts, 85, 124*nn5–7*, 124–
  25*n9*
Means, Mrs. (wife of R. A. Means),
  38, 130–31*n9*
Means, Rev. R. A. (president of Co-
  lumbus Female Institute), 8, 130–
  31*n9*
Memphis, Tenn., 92, 97, 100, 103,
  104, 110, 111; battle of, 134*n35*
Merrills (Merrilies), Meg, 87, 136*n47*
Middlebury Female Seminary, 7, 124–
  25*n9*. *See also* Willard, Emma
Milly, 8–9, 18, 37–39
Minnesota, 110
Minnesota Board of State Capitol
  Commissioners, 4
Minnesota Historical Society Research
  Center, 4
Minnesota Office of Vital Statistics, 5
Mississippi, 17, 18, 60, 135*n37;* seces-
  sion of, 133*n25*
Mississippi Central Railroad, 92
Mississippi Industrial Institute and
  College. *See* Mississippi University
  for Women

Mississippi River, 11, 103, 105,
  134*n35*, 136*n49*
Mississippi State College for Women.
  See Mississippi University for
  Women
Mississippi University for Women,
  125*n10*, 130
Mobile, Al., 45, 47
The Moderator (Union boat), 110
Montgomery, Al., 33, 35
Moore, Mr., 49
Morgan, John Hunt (Confederate
  general), 115, 137*n54*
Mount Equinox, 56
Mount Vernon, Va., 28
Murdock, Abram, 28, 34, 51, 130*n1*
Myerhoff, Barbara, 129–30*n27*

Nash, Maria (half-sister of Anne), 44,
  45, 131*n13*
Nashville, Tn., 64, 134*n30*
Neault, Carolyn, 126–27*n14*
New Orleans, battle of, 68, 69,
  134*nn35–36*
Newport News, Va., 133*n28*
New York, 28
New York City, N.Y., 114, 115
North Carolina, 44, 45, 132*n23*,
  133*n25*
Nye, Edith Seabury (daughter of
  Channing), 14, 124*n5*, 127*nn16*,
  18

Oakland Cemetery, 5, 14, 127*nn16,19*
Odin, 113
Ohio, 137*nn53–54*

Panola, Miss., 83, 84, 85, 94, 96
Parish, Peter, 136*nn46,48*
"Peculiar Institution," 4, 8, 37, 44. *See
  also* Slavery
Pemberton, John (Confederate gen-
  eral), 135–36*n42*
Pensacola Bay, S.C., 60, 133*n26*
Personal Narratives Group, 129–30*n27*
Petersburg, Ga., 126*n14*

Petersburg, Va., 28, 130*n2*
Philadelphia, Pa., 25
Pickens, Fort, battle of, 60, 133*n26*
"Piecing and Writing," 123–24*n3. See
also* Showalter, Elaine
Pittsburgh Landing, battle of, 134*n32.
See also* Shiloh, battle of
Pizziferri, Shirley, 124*nn5,7*
Plimpton, Caroline (mother of Caroline Seabury), 6, 7, 124*n8*, 131*nn10,
18*
Plimpton, Edwin (uncle of Caroline
Seabury), 7, 10, 11, 13, 56, 61,
126*n12*, 132*n22*
Plimpton, Gershom (grandfather of
Caroline Seabury), 6
Plimpton, Maria (first wife of John
Seabury), 6, 11
Plimpton, Mary Chamberlain (wife of
Stillman Plimpton), 124*n8*
Plimpton, Mary Hastings (wife of
Edwin Plimpton), 7, 10, 11, 13,
126*n12*, 132*n22*
Plimpton, Oliver, 6
Plimpton, Stillman (brother of Caroline Plimpton), 124*n8*
Porter, David Dixon, 113
Potomac River, 27, 130*n2*
Preston, Madge: diary of, 19
Price, General, 84
Prime, Uncle, 79
"Proper Sphere," 18, 129*n24. See also*
Cult of True Womanhood; Welter,
Barbara
Protection Papers, 103. *See also* Loyalty Oath

"The Rebellion," 109
Reflexivity: defined, 129–30*n27.
See also* Myerhoff, Barbara; Ruby,
Jay
Richmond, Va., 28, 112, 130*n2*
Ropes, Hannah: diary of, 19
Rose (slave sold at auction), 40
Ruby, Jay, 129–30*n27*
Ruggles, Daniel (Confederate general),
99

St. Louis, Mo., 113
St. Paul, Mn., 11, 13, 14, 71, 111,
127*nn15–17,19*
St. Paul Dispatch, 127*n19*
St. Paul Pioneer, 117
Savannah, Ga., 132*n21*
Scott, Anne Firor, 124–25*n9*
Scott, Sir Walter, 136*n47*
Seabury, Austin (son of Channing and
Elizabeth), 14, 127*n16*
Seabury, Caroline Plimpton (mother
of Caroline Seabury). *See* Plimpton,
Caroline
Seabury, Caroline
—alone in the world, 17, 50, 54, 80–
81, 116
—birth, 6
—concern about the Civil War, 60–
65, 68–70, 74–77, 84–91, 93–94,
101, 103–104, 109
—death, 14, 127*n19*
—diary of, 4, 9, 11, 14–21, 123*n1*,
124*n4*, 127–28*n20*, 128*n21*
—education, 7
—attitudes toward faith and religion, 52–53, 58, 63–64, 80–81,
116
—family background, 6–7, 124*nn5–8*,
126*n12*, 130*n4*, 131*nn10,18*, 132*n22*
—hearing "Hard Shell Baptist Sermon," 71–73
—ideology of True Womanhood, 18–
19. *See also* Cult of True Womanhood; Proper Sphere; Welter,
Barbara
—journey from North to South in
1854, 3–4, 8, 25–36 *passim*
—journey from South to North in
1863, 11, 81–116 *passim*
—life in St. Paul, Mn., 11–14
—concerns about Martha, 45, 50, 51–
55
—Milly's beating, 8–9, 37–39. *See also*
Milly
—nursing boy through smallpox, 9,
47–51, 131*nn16–17. See also* Dupree,
John; Dupree, Mrs.

Index

Seabury, Caroline (*continued*)
— nursing Confederate wounded, 66–69
— places of residence, 124*n8*, 126*n13*, 127*nn15–16*
— racial prejudice of, 18, 28–29
— attitudes toward slavery, 8–9, 17–18, 28–29, 31–32, 45, 55–56, 59–60, 85–86, 114
— auction of Suey, 41–43. *See also* Suey
— teaching at Columbus Female Institute, 3, 7, 8, 10, 18–19, 125*n10*, 126*nn11–12*, 130*n8*, 135*n37*
— teaching at Waverly, 10, 70–71, 75–76, 79–81, 126–27*n14*, 131*n12*, 135*n37*. *See also* Waverly; Young, George Hampton
— as woman teacher, 3, 4, 6, 7, 8, 17, 18–19
Seabury, Channing (brother of Caroline), 4, 6, 7, 11, 12, 13, 14, 20, 57, 63, 110, 124*nn6,8*, 126*n12*, 127*nn15–16,18–19*, 132*n22*
Seabury, Charles (son of Channing and Frances), 13, 127*n15*
Seabury, Elizabeth Austin (second wife of Channing), 13, 14, 127*nn16, 18*
Seabury, Gerald (son of Channing and Elizabeth), 14, 127*n16*
Seabury, Helen (sister of Caroline), 6, 124, 131*n18*
Seabury, John (brother of Caroline), 6, 131*n18*
Seabury, John (father of Caroline), 6, 7, 131*n18*
Seabury, John (son of Channing and Frances), 13, 127*nn15–16*
Seabury, Joseph (grandfather of Caroline), 6
Seabury, Julia (half-sister of Caroline), 6, 131*n18*
Seabury, Lucretia (half-sister of Caroline), 6, 131*n18*
Seabury, Maria (half-sister of Caroline), 6, 131*n18*

Seabury, Martha (sister of Caroline), 6, 7, 9, 15, 16, 37, 45, 47, 50–53, 55, 57, 58–59, 63, 124*n8*, 126*n12*, 131–32*n20*
Seabury, Mary (sister of Caroline), 6, 131*n18*
Seabury, Paul (son of Channing and Elizabeth), 14, 127*n16*
Seabury, Rebecca (grandmother of Caroline), 6
Secession, 132*n23*, 133*n25*
Selma, Al., 35
Shakespeare, William, *Titus Andronicus*, 131*n14*; *A Midsummer Night's Dream*, 131*n15*
Shelley, Percy Bysshe, 39; "To A Skylark," 131*n11*
Shiloh, battle of, 65, 134*n32*. *See also* Pittsburgh Landing
Showalter, Elaine, 123–24*n3*. *See also* "Piecing and Writing"
Slavery, 4, 8, 11, 17, 37, 39, 44–45, 59, 114, 132*nn21,23*, 135*nn39,41*, 136*nn43,46*. *See also* "Peculiar institution"
Smallpox, 9, 47–51, 131*nn16–17*. *See also* Dupree, John; Dupree, Mrs.
Smith, Captain, 111
Smith, Miss, 27, 33, 34, 130*nn1,5*
Smith, Mrs., 33, 34, 36, 130*n5*
Smith Street (Brooklyn, N.Y.), 116
Snow, Mr. and Mrs. Robert Allen, 126–27*n14*
Southbridge, Mass., 3, 6, 115, 124*nn7–8*
South Carolina, 32, 61, 132*n23*, 132–33*n24*; secession of, 133*n25*
Southerners, 64, 132*n23*, 134*n31*, 136*nn48–49*
Springfield, Ill., 132–33*n24*
"Stars and Stripes," 107, 108, 109
Stedman, Dr., 111
Stephens, Alexander Hamilton (Vice-President of the Confederate States of America), 65, 134*n31*
Stone, Mr. (assistant in Caroline's escape), 11, 82–105 *passim*, 118

Stonewall Brigade, 133*n29*
Stowe, Steven, 129*n25*
Studies in Autobiography, 129*n27*
Suey, 18, 41–43
Sumter, Fort, battle of, 60, 133*nn25–27*
"Sunny South," 43, 47, 56, 64, 93
Sykes, Mr. ("Mr. S") (assistant in Caroline's escape), 84–107 *passim*

Tallahatchie River, 96
Teaching: at all-female schools, 123*n2;* as benevolent occupation for women, 124–25*n9;* curriculum of female academies, 124–25*n9;* percentage of female teachers in U.S. in mid-1800s, 123*n2;* as profession for women, 3, 18–19; role of female academy in perpetuating cultural values, 129*n25*
Tennessee, 132*n23,* 134*n30;* secession of, 133*n25*
Texas: secession of, 133*n25*
Thompson, Waddy, 36
Tombigbee River, 45, 126*n14*
Troy Seminary, 124–25*n9. See also* Willard, Emma
True Womanhood, Cult of. *See* Cult of True Womanhood
"Twenty Negro" Law, 135*n41*

Union army, 11, 61, 63, 65, 70, 76, 94, 99, 109, 110, 133*nn26,28–29,* 134*nn30,32,34–35,* 134–35*n36,* 135*nn39–40,* 135–36*n42,* 136*nn44, 48–49,* 137*n54*

Vaughn, Dr., 44
Venable, Judge, 77, 103
Vermont, 115, 116

Vicksburg, battle of, 10, 76, 81, 82, 90, 91, 98, 109, 112, 135*n40,* 135–36*n42*
Virginia, 70, 130*n2,* 132*n23,* 133*nn25, 29*

The Wanderer (slave ship), 55, 132*n21*
Washington, D.C., 14, 25, 27, 61, 127*n19,* 130*n2*
Waverly (Waverley) Plantation, 70, 75, 79, 80, 82, 126–27*n14,* 131*n12,* 135*n41*
Weldon, N.C., 29
Welter, Barbara, 129*n24. See also* Cult of True Womanhood; Proper Sphere
West Point, Miss., 75, 83, 84, 126*n14*
White Mountains, 56
Willard, Emma (founder of female academies), 7, 124–25*n9. See also* Middlebury Female Seminary; Troy Seminary
Wilmington, N.C., 30, 35
Wisconsin, 112
Woloch, Nancy, 123*n2,* 124–25*n9,* 137*n52*
Women Teachers on the Frontier, 124–25*n9. See also* Kaufman, Polly Welts
Women's Studies International Forum, 129*n27*
Women's Studies Quarterly, 129*n27*

Yankee(s), 27, 29, 30, 34, 64, 65, 68, 75, 79, 81, 82, 85, 86, 87, 89, 90, 91, 92, 93, 94, 99, 100, 101, 102, 103, 111, 135*n37,* 136*n49*
Yocona [Yokney] River, 93
Young, Anna, 135*n41*
Young, George Hampton, 126–27*n14,* 131*nn12–13,* 135*n41. See also* Waverly

Zacchaeus, 135*n38*